T0199145

Broken and Divided:
America and the Church

Waiting for God's Kingdom to Be Unveiled

JOCELYN WHITFIELD

WESTBOW
PRESS®
A DIVISION OF THOMAS NELSON
& ZONDERVAN

WestBow Press books may be ordered through booksellers or by contacting:

WestBow Press
A Division of Thomas Nelson & Zondervan
1663 Liberty Drive
Bloomington, IN 47403
www.westbowpress.com
1 (866) 928-1240

ISBN: 978-1-9736-3802-5 (sc)
ISBN: 978-1-9736-3803-2 (hc)
ISBN: 978-1-9736-3801-8 (e)

Library of Congress Control Number: 2018910099

Print information available on the last page.

WestBow Press rev. date: 11/14/2018

Dedication

To believers, pastors, faith leaders, and ministers who are hungry to see God's Kingdom come. And those who have not spared their lives and resources for the cause of Christ and the Great Commission. It is also dedicated to those who will step forward in this hour to light up this world with the Light of Christ to reveal God's Kingdom to the world.

Acknowledgement

I am thankful for my friends and families who have encouraged me and covered me in prayer as I struggled with writing this book.

I am also thankful to my friend, June Mickens, who helped with most of the editing, knows my heart and thoughts and who prayerfully sought God for direction in the writing of this book

Contents

Preface

God has spoken. He has given us our mission. We are to fulfill the Great Commission and take the good news of Christ worldwide, make disciples and multiply God's Kingdom of righteousness on the earth (Matthew 28:19-20). With that as our charge, we cannot remain silent when evil prevails. As Christ's Ambassadors and reconcilers, we not only have been given the authority to proclaim the good news that Christ offers as the path to God the Father; but are to speak on His behalf in the public square- to be the voice of reason in the midst of confusion and chaos.

We are His peacemakers. We represent Him, the Prince of Peace. We are authorized to bring His peace and presence into the world, given that His Spirit dwells in us. We must not forget, that we have been given a kingdom agenda by none other than the King of Kings.

Our executive orders come from the Creator, Himself, to represent Him and to carry His glory and light to a fallen world. We are conduits of His power and love, vessels of His grace and empowered by the Holy Spirit. We been called to carry the gospel of Jesus Christ to a world desperately looking for the light. This is the greatest calling of all.

Our instructions are clear. Our job has been defined. So why are we not listening and acting? So why are we failing at this, in America and even in other Nations throughout the world?

This book gives a fresh perspective on some of the reasons why we are failing at achieving the Great Commission and gives insight into ways in which we can accomplish what we have been charged to do.

Introduction

As we look at our world, our country, our lives, and our churches today, we see that there is a lot of shaking going on. There is chaos, confusion, death, destruction. There is the dismantling of governments, wars and the threat of wars, terrorism. There is racism and hatred rising in people's hearts and penetrating the fabric of society. We are mired down by lies, corruption, and unbelief in God.

We are living in times of uncertainty. You might say that everything that *can* be shaken *is* being shaken.

The enemy, Satan, has raised his head; he is spreading evil and causing havoc in the world—in the lives of believers and unbelievers alike. However, instead of a formidable earthly opponent, he faces only a weak Church. Signs that we have rendered ourselves impotent show up daily as we fail to express any outrage at the prevalence of evil in our world. We grow weaker by the day as we remain silent, though very aware of the ills and the needs that surround us. We are not serving as the shining lights of Christ in this dark world. Instead, we stand by mute, and we simply watch.

So where is the Church of Jesus Christ today? Why is our voice silent?

To be truthful, I do not know. It appears as if the Church is doing very little to impact our world and country. Some mainly focus only on those issues that they care about. Even when we do speak, it appears that we have limited influence; few listens. Just recently, for example, our country experienced a loud outcry from more than a million youth, marching in cities throughout America and demanding action from our leaders over the senseless killing of students in their schools and local communities. Yet, voices from our churches have been strangely silent in calling out for justice, repentance, and moral changes in our laws. I cannot find the voice of Christ in the midst of all of this. Where is the clarion call for righteousness and responsibility? Why hasn't the Church sounded the alarm or responded?

The Bible tells us that nothing happens on this earth without God revealing it to His people first. According to Amos 3:7 (*NKJV*), "Surely the Lord God does nothing, unless He reveals His secret to His servants the prophets." Once that word is revealed to one person, it must be shared with others. Throughout Scripture we see that God instructed His people to set watchmen on the walls to stand guard for the children of Israel. The watchman's job was to patrol the designated area and to warn the people in case of danger. God told the prophet Ezekiel: "Son of man, I have made you a watchman for the house of Israel; therefore, hear a word from My mouth, and give them a warning from Me" (Ezekiel 3:17, *NKJV*). Similarly, God spoke through Isaiah: "I have set watchmen upon thy walls, O Jerusalem, which shall never hold their peace day nor night: ye that make mention of the LORD, keep not silence" (Isaiah 62:6, *KJV*).

Scripture also explains the consequences that follow when watchmen fail to do their jobs. "But if the watchman sees the sword coming and does not blow the trumpet, and the people are not warned, and the sword comes and takes any person from among them, he is taken away in his iniquity; but his blood will I require at the watchman's hand" (Ezekiel 33:6, *NKJV*).

The threat written about in Scripture is not simply something that occurred in biblical times; we see all around us that danger continues to be very real. If God's word is true, as we know it is, then He has revealed His secrets to someone, and those who receive His word are supposed to respond with their voice and sound the alarm. So, where are today's watchmen? Did they all abandon their posts? Where are the generals—the pastors, prophets, and ministers of the Most-High God? The old generals whose voices we once heard clearly—Billy Graham, Martin Luther King, and others—have passed on. Are there none left now that these are gone? Are there any voices to be heard regarding the trouble that threatens our current world, or are today's voices merely relegated to the safe confines of our churches? Who is speaking for God in this world?

If the truth be told, each of us in the Church of Jesus Christ is to be His watchman and spokesperson. We each have been called to hear the voice of the Lord and then to use what we receive from Him to be an active messenger of righteousness and justice in our society.

The aim of this book is to awaken the Church to its call- *to be the Light and Salt of the world of the world and to fulfill the Great Commission.* We are representatives of Christ's kingdom; His voice, hands, and feet placed in a world that is desperately in need of His presence.

As you go with me on this journey, you may think that this book criticizes Christianity as it is today. You are right; in some ways it does just that. However, my purpose is not only to challenge your thinking about how you represent God in the world, but also to spur you to become a part of the biblical notion of the *Church*—the bride for which Christ will return one day.

Let me say that everything written here may not reflect your local church or your life as a believer. I know that there are some churches and believers who represent the kingdom in extraordinary ways and who labor incredibly for the cause of Christ. (I happen to attend such a church and know individuals who exercise great influence.) Sadly, though, if we are being honest, when we consider the state of our world, we must say that those having a great impact are in the minority. Nonetheless, wherever any of us stands today, I believe that there is still room for improvement.

You also may ask who I am, and why you should listen to me. Ultimately, you must decide for yourself whether you will take any of what I share here to heart. I offer simply that I am a member of the body of Christ—one who desires to see the Great Commission advanced and the ever-growing family of believers truly maturing and serving as activists for making the love and peace of Christ known in midst of our troubled world (Matthew 22:37-39).

In many respects I have written this book as much for myself as for you. My prayer for you as you read each chapter, and for me as I write, is that:

- We will come to know that receiving salvation through Christ, is not meant only intended to get us into heaven, but it is the beginning of our ministry on earth.
- We will put way the personal distractions that interfere with hearing and responding to the voice of the Lord and open our eyes to the truth by following through with obedience.
- We will understand clearly the incredible opportunity that has been given us to develop a relationship with the Lord of all and to fulfill His divine purpose.
- We will gain insight and the powerful revelation of who we are, whose we are, and our kingdom purpose.
- We will recognize some of the reasons why in some respects, the Church seems powerless and without influence today and discover ways we can reverse that tide.
- We will come to know the true meaning of worship- God's heart.
- We will begin to grasp what it truly means to be citizens of God's kingdom and how we may become the glorious Church for which Christ will return.
- We will come to understand that what the world needs now is the Love of God and we are to demonstrate His love unconditionally so that others may be drawn into the loving arms of Christ.
- We cannot achieve the commission that we have given by Christ without our reliance on the power of the Holy Spirit.

I hope that one day soon we can point to an endless list of watchmen, men women, and children who have taken hold of their divine assignment of *proclaiming the gospel, making disciples and ushering in the Kingdom of God- Christ's Church!*

Chapter 1

Why Everything Is Being Shaken ...

So, don't turn a deaf ear to these gracious words. If those who ignored earthly warnings didn't get away with it, what will happen to us if we turn our backs on heavenly warnings? His voice that time shook the earth to its foundations; this time—He's told us this quite plainly. He'll also rock the heavens: "One last shaking, from top to bottom, stem to stern." The phrase "one last shaking" means a thorough housecleaning, getting rid of all the historical and religious junk so that the unshakable essentials stand clear and uncluttered.

Do you see what we've got? An unshakable kingdom! And do you see how thankful we must be? Not only thankful, but brimming with worship, deeply reverent before God. For God is not an indifferent bystander. He's actively cleaning house, torching all that needs to burn, and [H]e won't quit until it's all cleansed. God himself is Fire!

—Hebrews 12:25–29 (MSG)

Look around. There is indeed a lot of shaking going on. In the world, there is trouble, such as earthquakes, hurricanes, floods, physical and data insecurity, and violence. And the list could go on. In our lives, there is trouble, such as health issues, strained families, divorce, financial struggles, and suicide. Even in the church of Jesus Christ, there is trouble: division, disunity, immorality, and confusion. We appear to be a broken and divided people who have lost our way.

Everything that *can* be shaken *is* being shaken.

It's interesting that the Bible forecasts some shaking. We see such a warning in the passage from Hebrews that opens this chapter. Jesus also spoke of the trouble that believers would confront. "In the world you will have tribulation; but be of good cheer, I have overcome the world" (John 16:33 NKJV).

So, it appears that the existence of shaking and trouble around us is not unexpected. In fact, it is happening for a purpose. Unanswered is why we, as Christ followers, seem to be experiencing so much shaking from within. What's more, why do we appear unable to share in our overcoming power and capacity of Christ through us to impact the world for good?

I believe a primary reason is that we have limited understanding of who we are, whose we are, and the Word of God. Until we are sure of our identity and what that means, we will never fully understand what our salvation has done for us nor will we be able to completely take hold of what we have been called to do. Also, it appears that far too many of us have slipped away from our first love and are living as if Christ is not the Lord of our lives. We have not submitted our lives to His control or authority and live as though we have not been given a mission to be fulfilled other than that within the four walls of the church.

It isn't that we are sitting idle, because most of us are busy working in the church. In fact, many of us are living Martha lives (Luke 10:38–42). Like Martha, we have gotten busy doing a lot, much of which may be good; however, in our busyness, we have not made growing in relationship with Christ and advancing His mission a priority. Though busy doing church work, we may miss what Martha's sister, Mary, treasured: time sitting at the feet of our Shepherd and King, engaging with Jesus, hearing directly from Him, and receiving His directions.

Somehow, in our work for Christ, it is possible that we have lost our focus on Christ is our Lord and that He has called us to join Him in His work of transforming the lives of men and women.

We are not alone with respects to losing our focus, many pastors and ministers also have lost their focus. Instead of focusing on the charge and commission given by Christ, they are more focused on building larger church facilities; monitoring congregation sizes; and hosting programs, conferences, and conventions. Again, these are activities that very well may be good. It all stops being good though when Christ is an afterthought—if a thought at all. It stops being good when our efforts relate little to our Great Commission charge of ushering new believers into the fold and helping brothers and sisters mature in their faith to live righteous lives and be lights that point others to Christ.

Upon careful examination we must admit that much of what we do has nominal eternal value and minimal impact on kingdom building. In other cases, we may be more wedded to our religious traditions, rituals, doctrines, and theologies than we are to the Christ, who is supposed to be at the heart of it all. We somehow miss, or have forgotten, that it is the power of the gospel alone to save souls and transform lives.

Any time we allow anything else to take what rightfully is God's place, we open ourselves up to a period of shaking so that the proper order can be restored.

Still another cause for the shaking that we are experiencing may be our lifestyles- the way in which we live. For many of us, our lives are indistinguishable from the lives of the unsaved world. Our families show no difference. Our performance at work does not reflect that we are laboring for the Lord (Ephesians 6:5). Our stances on positions and our voting records frequently do not reveal that we honor God, understand His truth, and pay attention to His priorities. Our treatment of people, especially those who are different from us, often lacks love and respect, even if their actions are contrary to biblical teaching.

As the Church and Believers, everything that we hold true seems to be shaking. Why? Could it be that God is causing the shaking to wake us from our slumber, complacency, or in some cases, stupor? Could this be the Spirit of God saying that it is time to do His business, expand His kingdom, give Him glory, shine His light, and be His army to demolish the strongholds of Satan?

Again, let me state that there are believers and local churches already doing much for the cause of Christ. I am not minimizing their efforts. There are people among us who are consistent and heartfelt in their efforts to fulfill Christ's mission. They and their churches are alive and full of the power of God. They are seeking to reach the unsaved, meeting the needs of the poor, and equipping believers. Yet far too often, this is not the case. We find believers attending church, busy serving in church, or simply sitting back and waiting for Christ's return. Too many of us are content just to make heaven our home, and that has become our entire kingdom objective. We fail to realize that spending all our time within the church walls is not what we have been charged to do by Christ. Jesus called us to become fishers of men (Matthew 4:18–20). Although, Jesus instructed His followers to await His return, He also instructed them to occupy until His return. Jesus used a parable to give them a clear understanding of this, as it was His style. He said.

> There was once a man descended from a royal house
> who needed to make a long trip back to headquarters
> to get authorization for his rule and then return. But
> first he called ten servants together, gave them each
> a sum of money, and instructed them, "Operate with
> this until I return." (Luke 19:12–13 MSG)

We, like the servants in the parable, have been given a job to do. We are to operate, or *occupy* as used in some Bible translations, until Christ returns. What are we to do while we wait? Christ's direction to us has not changed. He gave us the Great Commission; He has called us to join Him fully in His work. And perhaps He is shaking or permitting shaking to occur so that He can get us going.

So, what is stopping us from making His work and mission our priority? What has hindered us? We will discuss possible hindrances in the next several chapters.

It is my hope that this discussion will serve as a catalyst and vehicle for change. May it not only adjust the way we think but also alter our practices. May it help us to live on purpose—as overcomers. May it cause us to rise to God's standard for righteousness and bring the reality of God's kingdom to the earth as we allow Him to work through us to fulfill the Great Commission.

Chapter 2

Hindrances to Fulfilling the Great Commission

> If a commission by an earthly king is considered an honor, how can a commission by a heavenly King be considered a sacrifice?
>
> —David Livingstone

As followers of Christ, we have been given an assignment set by Christ Himself before His ascension into heaven. He gave His followers instructions that have come to be known as the Great Commission. This was recorded in the gospel according to Matthew.

> And Jesus came and spoke to them, saying, "All authority has been given to Me in heaven and on earth. Go therefore and make disciples of all the nations, baptizing them in the name of the Father and of the Son and of the Holy Spirit, teaching them to observe all things that I have commanded you; and lo, I am with you always, even to the end of the age." (Matthew 28:18–20 NKJV)

That was, and is, our charge. Operating under Christ's authority and through the strength of the Holy Spirit, the mission for believers is straightforward

- *Go.*
- *Make disciples.*
- *Baptize those converts in the name of God—Father, Son, and Spirit.*
- *Help them grow by passing on Christ's teachings.*

Remember, Jesus lived with His small group but three short years. During that time, those followers walked beside Him, watched Him, and were trained by Him. Then He sent them out to do what they had seen Him do. He expected them to continue and expand His work. They were to devote the rest of their lives to pointing people to God.

What a weighty responsibility for a group of ordinary people! Christ was aware of this. He knew that His original disciples—and we today—lack the ability to accomplish this charge in human strength. For that reason, He promised us the comfort, wisdom, and power of His presence as we move about and carry out the work given to each of us. He also assured all who love Him and keep His commandments that they would receive the abiding support of the Helper—the Holy Spirit. Through the Spirit of God, we are positioned to perform all that is set out for us (John 14:12-18). So, Jesus not only gave us our marching orders, He also put in place supports so that we could accomplish what we were given to do.

When you think about it, in many respects, that group of early believers was no different than we are. They were ordinary people. Some were learned; some were not. Some were wealthy; some were poor. Their races, nationalities, and backgrounds varied. Yes, some of them did see and touch Jesus. This is where they differed from us. As members of "The Way", as the early Church was called, they walked in authority and power and turned their world upside down. Throughout the Book of Acts, for example, we see that wherever they went, they preached the gospel, lives were transformed, people were healed, God was glorified, and the culture was changed. Although given the same authority and empowerment, the Church today, for the most part, has forgotten the power and authority that has been given them to turn this world upside- down for the cause of Christ. Instead, we appear weak, and powerless and at times governed more by fear than faith.

Clearly, if the early Church is to serve as our model, we must ask ourselves what is hindering us from doing what they did and even greater. Perhaps it is because we have lost something that was grasped by our brothers and sisters from the past. What did they have that we lack? We must ask ourselves why are we not operating with the same authority and power? Why are we only minimally fulfilling the Great Commission here in America today? In the next several chapters, we explore ten possible obstacles that may have hindered the Church's impact to fulfill the Great Commission and hampered the spiritual development of believers to be effective witnesses for Christ.

Chapter 3

Neglect of One of Our Greatest, Gift, The Holy Spirit (Hindrance #1)

How little chance the Holy Ghost has nowadays. The churches and missionary societies have so bound Him in red tape that they practically ask Him to sit in a corner while they do the work themselves.

~C.T. Studd

As we look at the lack of power and influence shown by the Church today, it is important first to examine what may be preventing us from fully exercising the authority and the power we are supposed to have. To begin, we look to Jesus.

The Power Source for Believers

For a minute, do not think of Jesus as fully God. Remember that He also was fully man and, as a man, He walked this earth and needed power just as we do. So, how did Jesus, in His humanity, receive power? The answer is found in the story of Jesus' baptism.

It came to pass in those days that Jesus came from Nazareth of Galilee and was baptized by John in the Jordan. And immediately, coming up from the water, He saw the heavens parting and the Spirit descending upon Him like a dove. Then a voice came from heaven, 'You are My beloved Son, in whom I am well pleased' (Mark 1:9-11, *NKJV*).

When Holy Spirit descended upon Jesus at His baptism, He was infused by The Spirit of God. Then, after emerging from the 40-day period of temptation that followed, Jesus' earthly ministry began.

When I look at Jesus' life, as shared in the Gospels of Matthew, Mark, Luke, and John, He was not powerless. He went from town to town teaching about the kingdom and delivering people from the influence of darkness. When He spoke, storms stopped, healing occurred, and the dead were raised. When He appeared on the scene, He changed the course of lives. He operated as a human, yes, but He did so with the authority of God (Matthew 7:29). He showed us how heaven touches earth through a human body.

Christ is our model for a good reason. He expected us to carry on in His footsteps after He returned to heaven. He shared this plan with the disciples. "Very truly I tell you, whoever believes in Me will do the works I have been doing, and they will do even greater things than these, because I am going to the Father" (John 14:12, *NIV*).

To continue His work would be a daunting, if not impossible task for a band of ordinary people. God knew that and made appropriate provision. The Apostle John recounts what Jesus said next:

> If you love Me, keep my commands. And I will ask the Father, and He will give you another advocate to help you and be with you forever—the Spirit of truth. The world cannot accept Him, because it neither sees Him nor knows Him. But you know Him, for He lives with you and will be in you (John14:15-17, *NKJV*).

We know that the Father answered "yes" to Jesus' prayer for His followers to receive the Holy Spirit. In fact, Luke records in the Book of Acts what he heard, experienced, and saw in the period following Jesus' crucifixion.

> And being assembled together with them, [Jesus] commanded them not to depart from Jerusalem, but to wait for the Promise of the Father, 'which,' He said, 'you have heard from Me; for John truly baptized with water, but you shall be baptized with the Holy Spirit not many days from now.'

★★★

> When the Day of Pentecost had fully come, they were all with one accord in one place. And suddenly there came a sound from heaven, as of a rushing mighty wind, and it filled the whole house where they were sitting. Then there appeared to them divided tongues, as of fire, and one sat upon each of them. And they were all filled with the Holy Spirit (Acts 1:4-5, 2:1-4a, *NKJV*).

Being filled with the Holy Spirit was more than an emotional time during a church service. They were filled with the Spirit so that they could go out and do even greater works than He, as an individual, could do (John 14:12). And, they did just that. They continued His work and two thousand years later, we stand where we do today.

The introduction of the Holy Spirit on the Day of Pentecost changed lives. Today, lives are still changed for those who accept Christ as Savior, receives the Holy Spirit and new life that He brings.

> Peter said, 'Change your life. Turn to God and be baptized, each of you, in the name of Jesus Christ, so your sins are forgiven. Receive the gift of the Holy Spirit. The promise is targeted to you and your

children, but also to all who are far away—whomever,
in fact, our Master God invites' (Acts 2:38-39, *MSG*).

Clearly, it is the presence of the Holy Spirit that makes the difference. According to the Bible, all followers of Christ are supposed to have the same resurrection power-the power of the Holy Spirit, that Jesus and the early believers had. The enormous power of the Holy Spirit is available to us today to make an impact upon our world, as it did in the early church, to counter the devil, and to contribute to establishing God's kingdom on earth. *If this is the case, why then are we not doing the same things that Christ and the early church did?*

If the Holy Spirit Gives Power, Where's Ours?

Our Misunderstanding of the Spirit: The How

If you are a believer, you have the Holy Spirit. You may not yet realize Who He is and His role in your life and the life of every believer. In fact, you may not have heard very much about Him because He is the most neglected and mistreated member of the Trinity. To most, He remains a mystery. He is seldom referred to as God, a member of the Trinity, or accepted as God yet He is one of the team members.

The Holy Spirit has the same divine nature as the Father and the Son and is equal to them. He is eternal, not having a beginning or ending (Hebrews 9:14). He is omnipotent, having all power (Luke 1:35). He is omnipresent, being everywhere (Psalm 139:7). He is omniscient, understanding and knowing all things (1 Corinthians 2:10,11).

He was present and active in the beginning in creation as God the Father and the Son. Scripture specifically says that, when the "earth was formless and empty, and the Spirit of God was hovering over the waters", God began to speak and create (Genesis 1:2, *NIV*). However, we often are content to ignore or gloss over this important person of our Triune God.

The Holy Spirit has been given to us by the Father to perform specific and essential functions in the life of every believer.

He is our personal representative of the Trinity on earth. He is the superintendent and administrator of the Church of Jesus Christ. He is our personal indwelling Spirit of God Who acts as Father and Jesus's interpreter, revealer, and reminder of truth.

For example, He teaches us about the Father and about Jesus, and then He reminds us what we have learned at the appropriate times (John 14:26, 15:26). He highlights what is right and just (John 16:8). He shepherds us to the truth (John 16:13). He speaks to us on behalf of the Father, telling us what He wants us to know (John 16:13-14). He empowers us to be Christ's voice in carrying the gospel to the world (Acts 1:8). He serves as a guide, sometimes even blocking avenues that would be harmful to us or outside of God's specific plan at a given point in time (Acts 16:6-7). Because the Holy Spirit lives in us, He is our ever-present, internal connection to God.

Our lack of understanding about the Holy Spirit and His role in our lives, is not primarily our fault. Theologians and ministers often are both confused and confusing in this area. Some refer to Him as "an energy", "an anointing", or an "It". In some circles, for instance, the Spirit is portrayed merely as a mystical and impersonal force that comes upon people and causes them to do strange things— jump over pews, roll on the floor, scream loudly, or display other seemingly out-of-control emotional behavior. Perhaps that comes from a misreading of Scripture passages, such as the events recounted in Acts 2. There the Bible describes what occurred when the Holy Spirit first came upon the believers assembled together on the Day of Pentecost. The Sprit's anointing allowed this group of Galileans to speak in other tongues; what people sometime miss, though, is that those "tongues" were the languages of the unbelievers (Acts 2:6-12). Some of the onlookers thought the believers were drunk, but what they saw were people filled with the joy of the Spirit and out of their mouths they heard them tell of the greatness of God in their own languages.

So, yes, when we feel the Spirit of God in us, recognize Him working through us, it can be an extremely emotional experience, as it must have been for those referenced in Acts 2. People respond to the Holy Spirit differently. However, we must be careful not to mistake that emotion for the Spirit of God. Emotion may be one of the responses we have to what the Spirit is doing in and through us, but emotion is not the Spirit. For He is more than an emotion. He is the Spirit and power of God in us, working through us. Unfortunately, though, by misunderstanding who the Spirit is, or by presenting a limited view of how the Spirit and His gifts are manifested, we may miss His true benefit both in our own lives and, through us, to the world. In fact, we may discourage other believers from exploring or fully embracing the Spirit's ministry in their lives as they view us.

Our Misunderstanding of the Spirit: The Why

We know that the Holy Spirit is the power source of God for believers. But, how did we reach the point where He is the most neglected, underutilized, misrepresented, misunderstood, misused, and grieved member of the Trinity? There are reasons why we have arrived here.

Unlike Jesus, the Holy Spirit has not had a physical body to be viewed. He did not walk the earth. People did not see Him. He lives in us, and we are His body. The absence of a tangible person— someone whom we, or someone we know, can see or touch—can be a challenge. So, while we have eyewitness accounts about Jesus, and likewise we have Jesus' messages about what He has seen and heard from the Father, there is nothing comparable for the Spirit.

We also often overlook the Holy Spirit because He is seldom the subject of the teaching we receive today. How often are we instructed about the Holy Spirit in church services or Bible studies? I would guess that He is not on the Top 10 list for frequently covered topics over the past 5 years. Why is that so?

We are not taught about the Spirit because I find that many

ministers are uncomfortable talking about the Holy Spirit themselves because they may have limited understanding of the Trinity and the functions of its members. For that reason, it is easier, and safer, to stay away from the topic. Others may be well-learned—able to share what they have gathered from their teachers or the information available from commentaries, yet they lack a personal experience with Him. The unfamiliarity that follows from this absence of an intimate relationship causes them to shy away. Still other ministers may not teach on the Holy Spirit because they are grieving Him by their lifestyles (Ephesians 4:30).

The Apostle Paul taught believers about walking in the Spirit—a way of living that would allow us to be increasingly successful, day-by-day, by turning from harmful earthly habits and practices that hinder living out the fruit of the Spirit (Galatians 5:16-26; Ephesians 4:25-32). However, teaching about the Spirit, and about the fruit that will show as we are filled and walk with Him often shines a light on the areas of a minister's own life that are contrary to that very teaching.

Because people tend to avoid discomfort, especially if they are not ready for change, they steer clear of the convicting subject. Often the body of believers are left with limited knowledge of the Holy Spirit, His work in and through us.

The Power of the Spirit at Work

Without the Holy Spirit's working through us, accomplishing the Great Commission is not possible. It is His Spirit that draws people to Christ. If Jesus relied on the presence of the Holy Spirit in His life for power to undertake the earthly ministry that the Father gave Him, how much more do you and I need the Holy Spirit to be active and effective in ministry? Without Him we are incapable. He makes us able to take part in the work of the Kingdom. He makes clear to us what purpose God has in mind for us. We need His power for every aspect of the Great Commission—to go, to make disciples, to baptize them, and to instruct them in the things that we have been taught. We need Him, and the world needs Him as well. More than these we need Him in every in every aspect of living this Christian life. To not accept Him as God and be filled with His Spirit, we are likes ships in the water drifting without a Captain or a sail. Without depending on Him, we cannot accomplish what He has requested us to do. We also need the Holy Spirit to help us identify, strengthen, and use the spiritual gifts that He has given us to offer to the body of Christ for edification but also to help us serve as His ambassadors to the larger world (Romans 12:3-8).

Just think what would happen if the Holy Spirit's presence were evident in every believer. Picture the scene if the Holy Spirit's presence were made known in every church service. How many lives would experience God's transformative power and saving grace, the healing of sick bodies, the restoration of minds, and hear and be touched by God through the gifts of the Spirit. What if each encounter with believers and unbelievers alike, gave opportunity for them to experience the fruit of the Spirit -love, joy, peace, patience, kindness, goodness, faithfulness, and self-control (Galatians 5:22-23)?

I remember, when I was a young Christian, someone invited me to a Kathryn Kuhlman meeting. Kuhlman was an evangelist who came to speak in the area. This experience marked the beginning of my love affair with Jesus and the Holy Spirit. I saw this frail woman come on stage. The first thing she did was to the welcome the Holy Spirit's presence into the service. In her sermon she said that she would never step on stage if she did not have the Holy Spirit's presence going before her. At the service, people were saved, restored, and healed. That was truly my awakening to the presence and person of the Holy Spirit. This ordinary woman talked about her love for God—Father, Son, and Holy Spirit. More than that, she invited us to accept Jesus as Savior and to receive the baptism of the Holy Spirit. She was a human model for me of how the Holy Spirit could manifest His power through a life. Whatever she had, I wanted too. It was during this service that I lifted my hands up to heaven and opened my heart to the control of the Holy Spirit. Since then, He has been my daily companion and my power source for living.

Back on Track

So, what does it take for Spirit's presence to be known in us and in the life of the Church? It takes surrender.

We must be willing to surrender our lives, will, control, churches, and ministries to the Holy Spirit. We must give Him the honor and give Him His rightful place in each worship service and activity. He must be at the center of everything we do, whether it is the preached word, prayer, singing, the giving of tithes and offerings, or the use of the gifts of the Spirit in other ways. He knows our needs and, if we allow Him, will guide us in what we should say and do; He will show us how to direct our own affairs as well as the activities of our churches. And, if we follow Him, we will witness the miraculous. If we give Him control, He will fill us with His Spirit and anoint us to accomplish the Great Commission work we have been called to carry out—to evangelize the lost and to discern the needs of the people we are shepherding.

When we surrender our lives to the Holy Spirit, God's Word comes alive for us, and our minds are opened to receive His thoughts. Praise and worship erupt freely. Boldness and confidence appear as we proclaim the gospel and share our testimonies. The Spirit purifies our minds, hearts, and motives. We grasp the wonderful fact that we are not in ministry alone; we do not have to do God's work in our own strength, nor make decisions on our own, because the Spirit of the Lord is always with and in us.

When the Holy Spirit is released in our lives, we hear the voice of the Lord clearly. When we surrender to Him, Jesus is lifted, not us; people are drawn to Him and are able to receive this great gift of salvation. We do not have time to waste; there is so much work to be done. However, we must accept that we can accomplish nothing lasting in our own strength.

The Holy Spirit of God has been sent to be our advocate and helper. He waits for us to ask for His help and to surrender so that He can accomplish

His will. The Spirit is ready to release His anointing in us and through us to heal and deliver God's people and to save the unsaved. This is not the time to proceed on false emotion rather than the true Spirit. This is not the time to be reserved when we should be charged with His power to undertake the work we have been called to do.

This is not the time to shrink back because the mysteries of the Spirit seem too great or make us uncomfortable. This is not the time to allow ourselves to continue grieving the Spirit with our disobedience. Now is the time to passionately pursue His presence as never before so that He may manifest Himself to us and others.

If the Church of Jesus is serious about carrying out the Great Commission, the Holy Spirit will help us. Of all the gifts we have been given, except for Jesus Himself, there is none as precious and powerful as the Holy Spirit. Through Him, we get to experience God personally because His Spirit lives in us. We are in good hands—the hands of God, our Paraclete and advocate. Let's not waste this tremendous gift. We need Him, and the world does too.

Chapter 4

No Prayer, No Power (Hindrance #2)

The life of the church is the highest life, and its office is to pray. Its prayer life is the highest life, the most fragrant, the most conspicuous. When God's house on the earth is a house of prayer, then God's house in heaven is busy and powerful in its plans and movements. 'For Mine house shall be called an house of prayer for all people' (Isaiah 56:7), says our God. Then, His earthly armies are clothed with the triumphs and spoils of victory, and His enemies are defeated on every hand. … The very life and prosperity of God's cause—even its very existence—depend on prayer. And the advance and triumph of His cause depend on one thing: that we ask of Him.

~E. M. Bounds

Today's church lacks power. And, a powerless Church cannot carry out the Great Commission.

As we have seen thus far, every follower of Jesus has a built-in power source—the Holy Spirit. Sadly, although the Spirit lives within us, we may not have a close-enough connection to Him to access His great strength.

How do we make that connection? The answer is prayer.

There is an unmistakable connection between the Holy Spirit and prayer. Prayer touches the heart of God and moves Him to act on our behalf.

There is an old saying that remains true today: No prayer, no power. No matter how dynamic the praise and worship or how moving the teaching of the Word, no medium is as powerful as prayer. Nothing can advance the kingdom of God like it.

There was a time when no church would undertake any endeavor without first committing it to prayer.

As a youngster, I witnessed countless Wednesday and early Sunday morning prayer meetings where people came together

in homes and churches to pray, worship, and inquire of the Lord. Yet, today, prayer and fasting has taken a back seat to church activities. In our local churches, people do not come out for prayer services in the numbers as they do for meetings, special events, concerts, or Sunday worship services. Rarely do we hear of believers hunkering down in their prayer closets, interceding for others, or seeking God's guidance for solutions to the problems of the day.

Yet, we have a tool that has incredible potential to link us to our God, and we seem to do very little with it. Why?

What Is Prayer?

First, it would help to understand what prayer is and, perhaps, what it isn't.

The Billy Graham Evangelistic Association offers important insight into prayer:

> *Prayer is spiritual communication between man and God, a two-way relationship in which man should not only talk to God but also listen to Him.*

★★★

> *When you receive Christ into your heart, you become a child of God and have the privilege of talking to Him in prayer any time about anything.*

So, prayer has two parts. It involves us talking to God, and it also involves Him talking to us. As in any good relationship, there is an open exchange of communication; it is not a monologue.

Note that prayer is not reserved for major decisions or big events. The Bible tells us in Philippians 4:6 (*NIV*), "do not be anxious about anything, but in every situation, by prayer and petition, with thanksgiving, present your requests to God". We are invited to talk with God not about *some* things, not about *most* things, not about just *significant* things, but about *all* things. Through prayer, we can engage with God about every aspect of our lives—talking to Him and hearing from Him.

Prayer also is not about asking God just to rubber-stamp our wants or decisions. We certainly can, and should, ask things of Him. However, because His ways and thoughts are higher than ours, prayer allows us to ask God to interject His wisdom and plan into our situation, even if His will differs from ours (Isaiah 55:9; Matthew 26:36-46).

You see, prayer is a tremendous resource. It is the communication medium between our Father and us. It ushers us into an intimate relationship with Him which gives us access to His wisdom and opportunity to interact with Him in a highly personal way. As His children, we are welcomed at any time into the presence of Abba Father, our "Daddy" (Romans 8:15, Galatians 4:6).

What Happens When We Pray?

Something extraordinary happens when we pray. The supernatural power of God is released, heaven opens, His glory comes down, the angels listen, and we receive a response to our prayers. We sense the nearness of heaven and the Holy Spirit's presence. And there, in His midst, we experience the miraculous—new perspective, healing, freedom, and strength.

King David was a man of prayer and an excellent example for us. David utilized prayer throughout His life to communicate with God. He asked the Lord for guidance about how to respond to the challenges He faced. He often sought the Lord for wisdom, counsel, and direction. In 2 Samuel 5:17-21 (*NKJV*), for example, the Philistines, who were a constant enemy of Israel, pursued David to kill him right after his coronation as king. Instead of immediately waging war, David's initial move was to go to God in prayer. "'Shall I go up against the Philistines? Will You deliver them into my hand?' And the LORD said to David, 'Go up, for I will doubtless deliver the Philistines into your hand.'" And, God did indeed provide a victory. Though this is just one example, David routinely and freely exercised the gift and privilege of prayer. Rarely did he rely on his own wisdom or ability. He sought counsel (Psalm 34:4), gave thanks (2 Samuel 7:18-29), pleaded for mercy and asked forgiveness (2 Samuel 12:16), and engaged regularly with the God who is full of all wisdom and knowledge. In fact, as a testament to His connection with David, God said "I have found David the son of Jesse, a man after My own heart, who will do all My will" (1 Samuel 13:14, Acts 13:22, *NKJV*).

It goes without saying that Jesus modeled the lifestyle of prayer for us as well. Prayer was a constant in His life on earth. As the Son of God, He was in ongoing communication with the Father.

Scripture records numerous times when He slipped away from the crowds, and even from the disciples, to pray. Sometimes, it was before the sun rose: "Very early in the morning, while it was still dark, Jesus got up, left the house and went off to a solitary place, where He prayed" (Mark 1:35, NIV). At other times, He prayed in the evening and even all night: "And when He had sent the multitudes away, He went up on the mountain by Himself to pray" (Matthew 14:23, NKJV). Jesus modeled prayer at times of great decision (Luke 6:12-13) and during temptation (Matthew 26:36-46).

Jesus also prayed for Himself, for His disciples, and for those of us who would come after them (John 17). He prayed so intensely in the Garden of Gethsemane before His betrayal that out of his pores came blood and sweat (Luke 22:44). In His prayer time, He gained insight into pivotal decisions and strength to carry out the will of the Father. For Him, prayer was more than the recitation of rote verses or repetitive sayings; it was His time to talk earnestly with His Father.

Jesus spoke, and He listened intently for the Father's responses. Prayer was an essential part of His life on earth. Jesus wasn't selfish when it came to prayer; He didn't view it as a way that He alone could communicate with the Father. When the disciples asked Him for guidance about how to pray, He gladly taught them. Jesus offered an outline for prayer, which began with giving reverence to the Father for who He is, then asking that His will be done and that their needs be supplied (Matthew 6:5-15).

The apostles went on to utilize Jesus' prayer guide throughout their ministries. Not only did they adhere to the format given, these followers of Christ also embraced prayer as a significant component of their lifestyle. Throughout the book of Acts, we see the disciples praying together and mighty miracles of God being performed in response. On the Day of Pentecost, for instance, Jesus' followers gathered in the upper room, praying on one accord, and were filled with the Holy Spirit (Acts 1:12-14, 2:1-4). Because of what observers saw and heard from that newly empowered band of disciples, roughly 3,000 people were saved (Acts 2:41). Ananias, another of God's trusted servants, was praying privately when God directed him to go to Saul in Damascus, lay hands on him so that he could recover his sight and instruct him in the ways of Christ (Acts 9:10-19). When Peter was in prison, the people prayed, the prison doors were opened, and he was released (Acts 12:5-11). These are just a few of the instances of the early Church's reliance on prayer. Their connection to God was obvious.

The power of prayer is just as true today as it was then. When we pray, we communicate with our Father—the only one who truly has our best interest at heart, who knows the answers to our problems, and who is waiting to exercise His unmatched power to intervene in our situations.

It is through prayer that God can change the course of our lives, and it is through prayer that He can change the course of a nation.

In 2 Chronicles 7:14 (*NLT*), God commits that, "if My people who are called by My name will humble themselves and pray and seek My face and turn from their wicked ways, I will hear from heaven and will forgive their sins and restore their land." If we pray humbly and earnestly, God will move on our behalf. He will restore nations, churches, families, and lives that have veered from the path of righteousness. God desires to impact us in positive ways—to heal us—now and for eternity. The prayers of the saints are powerful, effective, and able to pull down strongholds (James 5:16-18). We must never underestimate the power of prayer, for nothing is impossible with God (Luke 18:27).

What Hinders Our Prayer Life?

Since prayer is vital to the life of a Christian. Why then does it seem that we do so little of it?

Busyness

A key reason for our lack of prayer may boil down to a single word: busyness. Most of us lead very full, and sometimes too full, lives. Jam-packed schedules can overshadow prayer time. In our busyness, it is easy to forget the God who should be the source of our strength both to do what we do and to address the problems we face. Charles
Haddon Spurgeon summed up what many of us experience:

> We do not forget to eat: we do not forget to take the shop shutters down: we do not forget to be diligent in business: we do not forget to go to our beds to rest: but we often do forget to wrestle with God in prayer, and to spend, as we ought to spend, long periods in consecrated fellowship with our Father and our God.

Fear of No Answer

Sometimes, we don't pray because we don't think that God is listening or that He will answer. However, that is not what Scripture teaches.

"Now, this is the confidence that we have in Him, that if we ask anything according to His will, He hears us. And if we know that He hears us, whatever we ask, we know that we have the petitions that we have asked of Him" (1 John 5:14-15, *NKJV*). "You will call upon Me and go and pray to Me, and I will listen to you" (Jeremiah 29:12, *NKJV*). "Continue earnestly in prayer, being vigilant in it with thanksgiving" (Colossians 4:2, *NKJV*). "Pray without ceasing" (1 Thessalonians 5:17). Clearly, we would not be encouraged to pray if God does not intend to hear and respond. He invites us to communicate with Him. We have permission to come boldly to the throne of grace so that we can interact with God and receive the Lord's favor.

> *Now that we know what we have—Jesus, this great High Priest with ready access to God—let's not let it slip through our fingers. We don't have a priest who is out of touch with our reality. He's been through weakness and testing, experienced it all—all but the sin. So, let's walk right up to Him and get what He is so ready to give. Take the mercy, accept the help (Hebrews 4:14-16, MSG).*

Look closely at these two passages.

1. As we saw earlier from 2 Chronicles 7:14, if we come to God in humility, He hears us. Similarly, James noted that the "prayer of a person living right with God is something powerful to be reckoned with" (James 5:16, MSG). So, we must come to God in the right spirit as we pray.
2. We can be assured that we will receive an answer to our prayers when we are seeking His will (1 John 5). In other words, when we earnestly want to know what God wants for us and are attempting to align our requests with His will, we can come into the Lord's presence, ask freely, and be sure that He's listening and will answer.

3. When we approach God in the right spirit, He's free to pour into us, guide us, and teach us. When we come just wanting God to give us what we want, we show that we're not open to instruction, and we miss so much that He otherwise would share.

Uncertainty about What to Say

Another reason why people may not pray as often is not knowing how or what to pray. The disciples experienced this challenge as well. To help them, Jesus offered guidance about prayer in Matthew 6. There, He shared insight about the heart and motives they were to have in approaching the Father (vv. 5-7). He also offered a sample format that included adoration, submission, petition, confession, deliverance, and praise (vv. 9-13). Jesus' help for the disciples is just as valid for us today.

However, God also knows that, sometimes we need additional support. Sometimes it is hard to put our feelings into words to express to God what is on our hearts. The Bible tells us that one of the functions of the Holy Spirit is to help us when we pray.

> *If we don't know how or what to pray, it doesn't matter. The Spirit does our praying in and for us, making prayer out of our wordless sighs, our aching groans. He knows us far better than we know ourselves, knows our pregnant condition, and keeps us present before God. That's why we can be so sure that every detail in our lives of love for God is worked into something good (Romans 8:25-28, MSG).*

How can believers always pray as the scripture instructs (Ephesians 6:18)? We can depend on Him to lead us in prayer, to connect us to the Father, and even to interpret what's on our hearts to God. All we must do is ask Him for help. However, if we are disconnected from the Holy Spirit, we miss out on this aspect of our prayer life.

Before moving on, let me share a bit about speaking in tongues while praying in the Spirit. This dimension of praying is rarely talked about and frequently is misunderstood when it is discussed.

Praying in tongues is different than the tongues discussed in Acts 2. There, those who received the Holy Spirit on the Day of Pentecost and were miraculously able to communicate with observers in the observers' native languages to spread the gospel despite language barriers. Instead, the Apostle Paul, in 1 Corinthians 12, outlines a variety of spiritual gifts that are present within the Church, and among those gifts are the ability to speak in tongues and to interpret tongues that are spoken in public (1 Corinthians 12:10). God has dispensed different gifts to the body of believers. The message is that everyone who is saved will receive one or more gift from the Spirit, but we all will not have the same gifts (1 Corinthians 12:6, *NIV*).

At other times, people do quite peculiar things while supposedly in the Spirit, or multiple people speak out in unknown tongues at the same time. However, this too is inconsistent with what the Bible says about being filled with Spirit. The Bible addresses order in church gatherings and notes that use of a spiritual gift *outside* of a person's private prayer space must help to build up those assembled (1 Corinthians 14:6-40). Thus, because people, on their own, will not understand the message delivered by someone speaking in tongues, there also must be an interpretation—another spiritual gift—so that those hearing may be edified. If there is no interpreter, the gifted person is to remain silent and keep the exchange private between him or her and God (1 Corinthians 14:26-28). Unfortunately, what we see at times, instead, are people who lack understanding of how God's Spirit actually is manifested in believers, and because of their misinformation, they often add the flesh and emotionalism to a gifting which is strictly spiritual and supernatural.

It is important to understand that speaking in tongues is also for our personal and private use. Scripture says that "he who speaks in a tongue does not speak to men but to God, for no one understands him; however, in the spirit he speaks mysteries" (1 Corinthians

14:2, *NKJV*). This dimension of praying is rarely talked about and yet when it is, it is misunderstood. In my personal prayer time, sometimes I speak in tongues. During these times of prayer, I feel at one with God; I can hear Him clearly. I can discern His work of grace in me. As I surrender control, His Spirit envelopes me and give voice to my prayers.

We need not fear the baptism of the Holy Spirit and receiving our private prayer language (tongues). Jesus said this.

"Now suppose one of you fathers is asked by his son for a fish; he will not give him a snake instead of a fish, will be? Or if he is asked for an egg, he will not give him a scorpion, will he? If you then, being evil, know how to give good gifts to your children, how much more shall your heavenly Father give the Holy Spirit to those who ask Him?" (Luke 11:11-13).

Our Father will never give us anything to hurt us. He is a good God Who only gives good gifts. Our prayer language is another one of His gifts that He gives us to communicate with Him. So, when you ask Him for the baptism of Spirit, you can be confident that this experience is a good one and it will be beneficial to you. According to 1 John 5:14-15 (*NKJV*), "this is the confidence we have in Him, that if we ask anything according to His will, He hears us. And if we know that He hears us, whatever we ask, we know that we have the petitions we have asked of Him". He always answers prayers that agree with His will.

Evangelist Reinhard Bonnke once said that the gifts of the Spirit "are not badges of honor but tools for the job". I agree wholeheartedly. The ability to speak in tongues is a gift. It is a tool. It is powerful and life-changing when used reverently in our prayer lives. Either way, whether in tongues or English, when a person prays in the Spirit, there is an opportunity to connect with the Him.

Back on Track

There is no magic formula or number of steps required for God to hear a prayer. We need not include repetition or eloquent words to get God's attention. All we need to do is communicate with Him openly, honestly, and humbly. Prayer is our communication tool with God; we share our hearts with Him, and it is one way that He communicates His commands, direction, perspective, plans, and more to us. We can be confident that, when we pray, heaven is open to hear us and respond.

Let's get personal. Is your faith weak? Do you lack direction, purpose, or love? Are you making a significant contribution to advancing the Great Commission? If not, how often do you communicate with the Father? How often do you both speak humbly and reverently to Him and then listen openly and with anticipation to what He has to say in return? Do you desire greater peace in your life? Do you long for the power of God to work in and through you? Then I urge you to take prayer seriously. When Jesus talked about prayer, He did not say "and *if* you pray..." but "*when* you pray..." He expects you and I to pray.

If you want to be a powerful witness for the cause of Christ, there is no greater vehicle than prayer. It really is true: No prayer, no power.

Chapter 5
A House Divided (Hindrance #3)

There is something sadly wrong when it is more important to us whether others are a part of our denomination, rather than whether they repent of sin, believe on Christ and live holy lives.

~J. C. Ryle

The only Christ that people view is the Christ that we present. As they stand back and watch us, many are asking what is this "church thing" about? They see a Church divided and broken -divided along denominations, doctrines, traditions, and rituals.

Scripture tells us that every kingdom divided against itself is brought to desolation, and every city or house divided against itself will not stand" (Matthew 12:25, NKJV).

Here, Jesus' own words explain the negative impact that division has on an entity. Applied to a city, a house, or otherwise, the outcome remains the same: Division eventually leads to destruction. So, what are the factors dividing Christ's Church, the body of Christ, especially in America? More importantly, how can we get back on track?

All that Divides Us

One of the things that has caused division in Christ's Church has been denominationalism. It has divided Christ's Church into religious groups and segregated them on the basis of different designations, church affiliations, different doctrines, sects and schools of thoughts. Often these groups are distinguished by beliefs, practices, creeds, confessions, and/or names that differ from each other.

In these groups, frequently believers are more wedded to their earthly pastors than they are to their kingdom purpose. So why is this problematic? Doesn't each denomination proclaim the gospel? Yes, most do. However, when the denomination becomes greater than the cause of Christ, the gospel, it is divisive. It becomes confusing to believers and unbelievers who are searching for a relationship with God. It also causes churches to operate in silos, separating the collective body of believers therefore making the Church impotent and ineffective and achieving the Great Commission.

The Apostle Paul encountered a similar situation among the believers in Corinth. The divisions there were so rampant that he strongly addressed the subject in his first letter to that church.

> *Now I plead with you, brethren, by the name of our Lord Jesus Christ, that you all speak the same thing, and that there be no divisions among you, but that you be perfectly joined together in the same mind and in the same judgment. For it has been declared to me concerning you, my brethren, ... that there are contentions among you. Now I say this, that each of you says, 'I am of Paul,' or 'I am of Apollos,' or 'I am of Cephas,' or 'I am of Christ.' Is Christ divided? Was Paul crucified for you? Or were you baptized in the name of Paul (1 Corinthians 1:10-13, NKJV)?*

As Paul noted, that the divisions were the results of individuals placing men and teachings above Christ who through His death and resurrection made salvation available to us all. No matter how well-meaning the Corinthians may have been, or we are today, some of us find ourselves more influenced by men and church doctrines than the written Word of God. Scripture tells us the traditions and doctrines of men can make the word of God of no effect—essentially, we can muddy the water to such an extent that we weaken the impact of the gospel. Again, as penned by Paul to the Corinthian church:

> *God didn't send me out to collect a following for myself, but to preach the message of what He has done, collecting a following for Him. And He didn't send me to do it with a lot of fancy rhetoric of my own, lest the powerful action at the center—Christ on the cross—be trivialized into mere words (1 Corinthians 1:17, MSG).*

God's Desire ... Unity

Let me clearly state that I am not attacking any specific denomination ... or your denomination. Whether we are dealing with 30,000 denominations or two, the point to be made is that Christ never intended for there to be a breach in His Church. Nowhere in Scripture will you find the term denomination. In fact, Jesus prayed for just the opposite.

Just before His betrayal and arrest, Jesus had some alone time with His disciples and He offered this prayer. After praying for Himself and the disciples, He prayed for all believers. On His heart was unity.

> *I do not pray for [the disciples] alone, but also for those who will believe in Me through their word; that they all may be one, as You, Father, are in Me, and I in You; that they also may be one in Us, that the world may believe that You sent Me. And the glory which You gave Me I have given them, that they may be one just as We are one; I in them, and You in Me; that they may be made perfect in one, and that the world may know that You have sent Me and have loved them as You have loved Me (John 17: 20-23, NKJV).*

Christ knew that the reliability of His message of salvation would be evident to the world only if the world could see His church unified, loving each other regardless of racial differences, fulfilling His mission, and carrying God's grace to the world.

Back on Track

As believers- Christ's Church, we cannot let denominational differences or religious traditions separate us. We are the body of Christ. If our rituals, values, and doctrines do not line up with Scripture and the promotion of unity among believers, then we must be willing to let them die.

Whether carrying the name Baptist, Methodist, Episcopalian, nondenominational, or something else, above all, we first are Christ's Church. Nothing should come before Him. There is not a valid reason that Christ's Body should be divided. If Christ is not divided, then why should we, His Church, be divided? The answer is that we shouldn't be.

Paul raised the subject of unity in strong terms once again in his letter to the church at Ephesus. His message to them is just as relevant to us today.

> *You were all called to travel on the same road and in the same direction, so stay together, both outwardly and inwardly. You have one Master, one faith, one baptism, one God and Father of all, who rules over all, works through all, and is present in all. Everything you are and think and do is permeated with Oneness. Ephesians 4:4-6 The Message (MSG)*

Also, we must recognize the source of division—Satan. If he can get us competing with one another, thinking that our group is superior to others, not loving one another, then he will use the divide-and-conquer tactic, and we will always be defeated as the Church.

On the other hand, when we unify around Christ, who is our core, nothing can derail us from achieving what we have been called to do and nothing can stop us from fulfilling the Great Commission.

This is not an impossible task. We have a Helper, the Holy Spirit. We need His help to keep us in the love of God and unity. We do not have to search far for His help. He indwells every believer and binds us together, enables us to live in harmony, and on one accord. Through Him, we are able, to diligently preserve the unity of the Spirit through His divine enablement (Ephesians 4:3).

Unbelievers will never believe that there is a Father who loves them and a Son who has died for them unless they first see the love of God in us who bear His name.

Imagine what impact we could have on this world for the cause of Christ if the Church walked in unity, with one mind, on one accord, loving one another and strongly demonstrating the character of Christ. Can't you just see the consolidated body of Christ, standing together for righteousness and proclaiming the gospel? Think how we could really advance the Great Commission if we truly committed ourselves to the Spirit and through Him, demonstrate our love for one another and walk in unity despite our differences. Can't you see the awesome declaration of Christ's love and His Spirit living in us that this would show the world?

So, let us start breaking down the walls that separate us. Let us strip off anything that hinders our unity. Let us run patiently together, upholding our faith, keeping our eyes on Jesus, and thinking of Him only as we pursue the highest mission of all—His Great Commission. It is time to take seriously God's call to unity so that the world will see us as one, one in the Spirit and one in the Lord so that they will come to know that salvation comes in Christ and Christ alone. ... and come to know that salvation comes to us in Christ and Christ alone.

As a reminder to us that in Christ we are one, I would like to conclude this chapter with the following song.

We Are One in the Spirit
By Jason Upton

37

We are one in the Spirit
We are one in the Lord
And we pray that all unity
May one day be restored
And they'll know we are Christians
By our love, By our love
And all praise to the Spirit
Who makes us one

Chapter 6

Culture Mix-Up (Hindrance #4)

Many confuse the United States with the Church or the Constitution with the Bible. They feel that the good of the United States is the same as the good of the Kingdom of God. Some feel that the Constitution of the United States is as infallible as the Bible. However, one with wisdom notice[s] that some things are Kingdom principles and some are not.

~Gayle D. Erwin

As believers the bible teaches that we are to be *in* this world but not *of* this world and that we are not to love the world and the things it offers (John 17:14-16; 1 John 2:15).

The unmistakable message is that we are not to be conformed to or either adopt the culture of the world. There is something about the way the world functions, and about the way God wants His people to function, that do not align.

In fact, there's something about the culture of this world that is contrary to the culture of God's kingdom. What then is the difference, and why does it seem to matter? What is culture?

The Merriam-Webster Dictionary defines *culture* as:

(a) the customary beliefs, social forms, and material traits of a racial, religious, or social group; also: the characteristic features of everyday existence (such as

39

diversions or a way of life) shared by people in a place or time ★★★

(b) the set of shared attitudes, values, goals, and practices that characterizes an institution or organization ★★★

(c) the set of values, conventions, or social practices associated with a field, activity, or societal characteristic

The World's Culture and the Church

The Kingdom Culture is quite different from the world's culture. During Jesus' earthly ministry, He modeled and taught about His kingdom to those who would choose to follow Him. He taught about mores and standards based on a covenant between God and His people. The attitudes, values, and practices at the heart of this culture rest on the notions of love, forgiveness, and reconciliation. In this Kingdom culture, God would provide through His death and resurrection, a redemption plan and an opportunity for a new way of life, if we but choose Him. The Kingdom culture that Jesus talked about is not based on laws and policies; it is one that seeks to draw mankind into an intimate relationship with God through Christ.

Christ has given us a charge to carry God's culture to the world; His values, customs, attitudes, love and character.

Unfortunately, we have not done a good job with this charge. We must admit that today, the body of Christ often looks and acts no different than the rest of the world. I believe that unknowingly we have adopted the world's culture—its values, customs, and ways. I use the word unknowingly because I believe that we have been deceived by Satan to think that the world's ways are no different, if not better, than God's ways.

Because we are ignorant of God's Word about the way we should be living, we veer away from God's standards. We are also ignorant of Satan's devices and tactics. Our ignorance allows him to deceive us into believing that what is wrong is right and that what is right is wrong.

As a result, of our limited knowledge of God's Word, we find ourselves conforming to culture of the world.

How did we get here, though? When did we start looking more like the world than like Christ?

In many respects this is not anything new. God knew that the pull of the world would be a strong and constant battle. For that reason, He inspired Paul to encourage the saints in the church in Rome, and us, that we should "not conform to the pattern of this world, but to be transformed by the renewing of your mind. Then you will be able to test and approve what God's will is—His good, pleasing and perfect will" (Romans 12:2, NIV). The message was not that everything about the world is evil. However, Paul was alerting believers of the need to be on guard, constantly testing what is seen and heard against the Word of God.

As I look at where we are today, it appears either that the messages of *being in the world but not of the world,* either are not being shared with believers or we have stopped listening.

Even though there are churches on practically every corner, I fear that too many in the Church do not understand the kingdom message because they have not been taught. Neither are they taught how to live righteously and grow to full spiritual maturity in Christ.

When a person is a babe in Christ, he or she lacks the discernment to determine the differences between the Kingdom culture and the counter-culture simply because they have not been taught to know the difference. Unfortunately, this lack of discernment and knowledge contributes to the vast number of believers who never advance beyond spiritual infancy.

For these reasons, many of us look and act more like the world than the Kingdom of God because we do not understand how to live out their lives as Kingdom people or how to represent the kingdom in connection with the state of our world. There are so many issues confronting us today—all which impact God's creation in one way or another and therefore touch the heart of God. We cannot highlight only one or two as "major" issues and thumb our noses at the rest.

41

As we follow Christ by advancing a kingdom culture, we must actively work, or at least pray for and support others who are actively working, to find solutions to issues across the board—issues that are eroding the fabric of society, issues that show our lack of care for one another, issues that separate people from God. The world needs to hear the voices of the righteous serving as a clarion call for justice and redemption ... anywhere and everywhere that call is needed.

Moreover, there exist confusion about what the Great Commission is. This is evident since most of the activities of the church or Kingdom work mainly resides inside the doors of the local church. Carrying the message to the community, or even efforts to equip believers to share the message in their daily circles, is only a small part of most church agendas ... if it happens at all. Our calling involves much more than what we do within the four walls of the church. The Great Commission charge is to go to all nations (Mark 16:15)—something we can't do if we stay in our church cocoons.

That assignment doesn't involve only foreign missions. We have been gifted and positioned by God to occupy every sector of society. No matter what our occupation or circle of influence might be, we are to shine God's light right where we live and work each day. We are to put into practice the values, beliefs, and actions that underscore our kingdom culture not only within the church building but wherever we go.

Yes, we must shine God's light, but we also are to bring His truth. There may be some discomfort in doing that—standing and sometimes being the lone voice of justice during the crowd. The world's culture—family, neighbors, friends, coworkers, politicians, the media, entertainers, and more—may point one way, but if God points another way, that is the direction we must pursue as His Church.

We cannot follow the world if doing so opposes Scripture. To do so, we dishonor God and become ineffective witnesses for the cause of Christ.

Trust me; going God's way, rather than man's way, may bring persecution. It may not be easy, but in the end, its brings great Kingdom results. As He prayed for the disciples and us, Jesus said this. He said. "I have given them Your word; and the world has hated them because they are not of the world, just as I am not of the world" (John 17:14, *NKJV*).

Jonas Clark writes that the Kingdom of God's culture is a war for dominion, kingdom against kingdom, values against values, truth against lies, and light against darkness."

That does not mean that everything we see and experience in the world is bad, however, it is important that we understand that when God's view conflicts with the world's opinion, and we choose the kingdom way, there may be hostility as a result. After all, the gospel is often an offense to unbelievers (1 Peter 2:7-8). When faced with opposition because we stand for God's culture, *relying on the Holy Spirit's comfort and the support of other believers* becomes so important. Our resolve is renewed, and we are strengthened to continue when we connect with the Holy Spirit and fellow believers.

We must remind ourselves of who we are and Whose we are. We are Christ's agents of transformation for these times, His spiritual compasses in the world, and the illuminators of His light and the kingdom way of living.

Back on Track

Is it possible, then, for the Church to get back on track as it relates to the issue of culture? Definitely.

A first step for us is coming to understand that kingdom culture is dynamic and powerful. If the Church truly were to grasp what is available to us in God, our decision making would be easier. The Apostle John wrote:

> *Don't love the world's ways. Don't love the world's goods. Love of the world squeezes out love for the Father. Practically everything that goes on in the world—wanting your own way, wanting everything for yourself, wanting to appear important—has nothing to do with the Father. It just isolates you from Him. The world and all its wanting, wanting,*

wanting is on the way out—but whoever does what God wants is set for eternity (1 John 2:15-17, MSG).

To get back on track, we also must be willing to examine and alter our schedules. Somehow, in our busyness, we seem to make time to learn and experience many things—to be influenced by a range of cultures—but we seem to lack time to become familiar with the culture of God.

We either have not learned, or we have forgotten, the formidable power that exists in the gospel to change lives, communities, and nations. We must be honest with ourselves. That the serious void of Christ-likeness and consciousness in our world has to do with the poor way we have represented Christ, as His ambassadors and that adopting the Kingdom culture has become second nature to us.

But, the good news is that the story need not end there. We can become a force for righteousness in this world and impact it for the good of God's Kingdom. *We can take God's Kingdom principles and lifestyle to the world and play a significant role in filling that gap and resolving America's problems.* We may be called to take that step as elected officials. Just as God prepared David, Nehemiah, Deborah, and others for office, He may be positioning some of us to serve as leaders in a similar way.

However, even if public office is not for us, we all are called to be ambassadors at the polls—prayerfully and responsibly choosing the men and women who will serve our nation, states, and communities. While not every candidate will be a believer, we are to ask God for discernment to identify those who do have a heart for Him; a character of respect; and an honest desire to collaborate with others, no matter their political affiliation, to serve mankind and to eek responsible solutions to the issues of the day.

Our work is not over once any election has ended. We are not to moan and groan about outcomes, nor are we to resist and thwart progress offered by anyone who was not our choice. We cannot blame the politicians entirely for the state of our nation and communities; we may have erred because we did not pray or listen and rely on the Lord to help us make such important decisions. No matter who has been elected to a political office, we are to continue in prayer. Apostle Paul wrote this to Timothy.

> *The first thing I want you to do is pray. Pray every way you know how, for everyone you know. Pray especially for rulers and their governments to rule well so we can be quietly about our business of living simply, in humble contemplation. This is the way our Savior God wants us to live (1Timothy 2:1-3, MSG).*

Finally, as we think about where we go from here, we must "be strong in the Lord and in the power of His might" (Ephesians 6:10, NKJV). *Having put on God's armor, we must stand firm and not allow ourselves to be hoodwinked, deceived, or beguiled by the devil (Ephesians 6:13).* We must not allow hardship, the promise of power, visibility, friendship, prosperity, support for our issues, or anything else to sway us from what we know to be right in the eyes of God. As the Apostle Paul wrote:

> *We refuse to wear masks and play games. We don't maneuver and manipulate behind the scenes. And we don't twist God's Word to suit ourselves. Rather, we keep everything we do and say out in the open, the whole truth on display, so that those who want to can see and judge for themselves in the presence of God.*
>
> *If our Message is obscure to anyone, it's not because we're holding back in any way. No, it's because these other people are looking or going the wrong way and refuse to give it serious attention. All they have eyes for is the fashionable god of darkness. They think he can give them what they want, and that they won't have to bother believing a Truth they can't see. They're stone-blind to the dayspring brightness of*

the message that shines with Christ, who gives us the best picture of God we'll ever get.

Remember, our message is not about ourselves; we're proclaiming Jesus Christ, the Master. All we are is messengers, errand runners from Jesus for you. It started when God said, 'Light up the darkness!' and our lives filled up with light as we saw and understood God in the face of Christ, all bright and beautiful (2 Corinthians 4:2-6, MSG).

We must stand up for Christ and His justice, peace, and righteousness.

We did not receive this new life, born of God's Spirit, to mix it up with a corrupt system that does not honor God. Just as Christ, during His time on earth, challenged the culture of the world, and even at times the culture within the church, we too have been called to speak up when the world's systems seek to overshadow the culture of the kingdom.

God provides a standard of righteousness—a moral compass for the world to see. We—His Church—have been selected to demonstrate God's standard to the world by serving as conduits of His love and power. *We were not reconciled to God, through the blood of Jesus Christ, to compromise our morals and to settle for lesser life. Instead, we are to serve as Christ's ambassadors—representing Him to the world along with the values, standards, beliefs, and all the rest that comprise His culture (2 Corinthians 5:20).* By directing us to go into "all the world", Christ told us that our mission is to influence every sector of society (Mark 16:15).

Chapter 7

My Skin is ... : Racism and Acceptance (Hindrance #5)

I refuse to accept the view that mankind is so tragically bound to the starless midnight of racism and war that the bright daybreak of peace and brotherhood can never become a reality. **★★★** *I believe that unarmed truth and unconditional love will have the final word.*

~ Dr. Martin Luther King, Jr.

Sadly, racism and racial division are still alive in the world. Sadder still, racism and racial division are alive in the Church.

In March 1968, Rev. Martin Luther King, Jr. called Sunday mornings at 11:00 the most segregated hour of the week in Christian America. Yet, some 50 years later, true diversity in our churches remains rare. Yes, there are a handful of churches that are putting forth serious effort to be inclusive and diverse; they carefully make staff and leadership decisions to ensure that they have varied racial and/or ethnic representation among parishioners and participants alike during worship services, and they are on the right track in doing so. *These churches have something to teach us all. However, even in those bodies, we find that, outside of time at church, seldom do believers break bread or fellowship together across races and ethnicities, unless they are on staff or in leadership.* And so, even where we are doing well, it appears that we, the Church, still have a way to go.

Racism and Diversity

As discuss the impact that race has had upon advancing the Great Commission, let's begin with the definition of racism and diversity. *Racism* can be defined as "the prejudice that members of one race are intrinsically superior to members of other races; discriminatory or abusive behavior towards members of another race". On the other hand, *diversity* implies that there is variety. "To have diversity, you need a mix of whatever you're talking about. ★★★ No matter what kind of diversity you're talking about, there needs to be a real mix, kind of like a huge box of Crayolas." (Vocabulary.com)

As we look at our churches, clearly most of them lack diversity.

Few houses of worship resemble a box of crayons on a Sunday morning. So, one of two things must be happening. Are we practicing racism—are we intentionally keeping away people who are different from us, making them feel unwelcome overtly or covertly in our churches through our words or behavior? Or, are we practicing carelessness—are we not investing time and effort to build diversity into the fabric of our home churches or, in the alternative, at least taking steps to partner with sister churches that represent other backgrounds and share with them regularly to bridge our racial and ethnic divides?

The idea of diversity in the Church is not a modern-day construct or civil-rights era platform. It is a biblical notion, and it is a part of Christ's assignment to us. So, it is no wonder why the Church is failing in advancing the Great Commission. We're missing opportunities to share the good news because, all too often, we remain separate from anyone who does not look like us.

The Great Commission and Race

Matthew's gospel referenced Christ's charge to "make disciples of all nations" (Matthew 28:19, *NKJV*). Mark couched it as an instruction to "[g]o into all the world and preach the gospel to every creature" (Mark 16:15, *NKJV*). In either recount, the message is clear:

Christ's intention was that the good news be shared with people across racial and ethnic lines. His gift of salvation is not just for one group of people; it is for all people.

If we look at Jesus' time on earth, we see that He practiced what He taught. He communed with people from different backgrounds; He engaged with them. Christ's willingness to break down divides—race, ethnicity, gender, age, class—was one of the things that made Him stand out and that drew people to Him.

Consider, for instance, Jesus' interaction with the Samaritan woman in John 4. The rift between the Jews and the Samaritans—a mixed-race people—was well-known. The Jews considered the Samaritans to be racial "half-breeds". For years, the two groups had been locked in a blood feud, divided by geography, religion, and race. They spewed venom at each other and protected their own turf. They disputed interpretations of Scripture and the proper way to worship. Neither group wanted anything to do with the other; in fact, Jews traveled out of their way to avoid going through Samaria and interacting in any way with *them*. Yet, the Bible tells us that, on at least one occasion, Jesus didn't take the long route around, as was the custom; He "left Judea and departed again to Galilee. But He needed to go through Samaria." (John 4:3-4, *NKJV*) Why? His unspoken intention was to engage with the people there, and that He did indeed. After sending the disciples away, supposedly to find food, He stopped at Jacob's well. A Samaritan woman appeared, and what began for her as a simple request from a man for a drink of water turned into a life-altering conversation for her and, through her, for an entire community (John 4:7-42). Jesus was willing to look beyond the fact that this was a woman, a Samaritan, and a person with a checkered lifestyle.

He disregarded social barriers and offered her forgiveness, redemption, and a new life. Even though His actions gave the disciples pause (v. 27), He modeled for them what it looks like to reach across barriers and to engage with people who are different. He showed them both how to share and how to live out the gospel regardless of social status, gender, or skin color.

Jesus passed the instruction of inclusion on to the disciples with whom He walked daily. He also passed that teaching on to us.

Racial Unity in the Early Church

We see a great deal of diversity in the group of people who were a part of the Way—that original group of believers. *On the Day of Pentecost, for example, when the gift of the Holy Spirit was given to those assembled and they began to proclaim the gospel, they were able to communicate with the many nationalities of people who were in the vicinity and intrigued by what was happening.*

> *Then they were all amazed and marveled, saying to one another, 'Look, are not all these who speak Galileans? And how is it that we hear, each in our own language in which we were born? Parthians and Medes and Elamites, those dwelling in Mesopotamia, Judea and Cappadocia, Pontius and Asia, Phrygia and Pamphylia, Egypt and the parts of Libya adjoining Cyrene, visitors from Rome, both Jews and proselytes, Cretans and Arabs—we all hear them speaking in our own tongues the wonderful works of God' (Acts 2:7-11, NKJV).*

Hearing their questions, Peter eloquently and persuasively explained what was happening. The Bible goes on to relay that "those who gladly received his word were baptized; and that day about three thousand souls were added to them" (Acts 2:41, NKJV). So, the *Church* started out as a multicultural body.

The Church's racial and ethnic diversity continued. The Apostle Paul, for instance, was a significant church planter and understood that all races and ethnic groups represent the body of Christ. He didn't start one church for Jews and one church for Gentiles. He ministered to churches in Rome, Galatia, Ephesus, Corinth, Philippi, and more, and he encouraged those bodies to worship and fellowship together and to support one another as they were able.

He understood that the gospel has the power to bring people together regardless of their race or ethnicity, and he worked tirelessly to cross boundaries to unite believers.

Although the early Church did well on many accounts, multiculturalism also brought challenges. One instance recorded in Scripture involves Peter and his team on a trip to Antioch (Galatians 2:11-16). It appears that the team was having a fine time, freely worshipping, fellowshipping, and communing with their Gentile brothers and sisters there. The trouble arose when some other Jewish brethren arrived and were horrified that the team was not strictly following the law—likely, and probably most noticeably, the dietary rules followed by the Jews. Peter and team, instead of pushing back on their detractors, backed away from their new Gentile brothers and sisters. And, Paul called them on it, especially Peter, who was the supposed to be the leader and the model of acceptance of diversity for the rest. Paul reminded them that they were to function based on Christ's grace and not the law.

Scripture's plain message is that, when we refuse to embrace other races and ethnic populations, it is an offense to God. When we discriminate against our sisters and brothers in Christ because of origin, we sin. As written by the Apostle Paul to believers:

> *For you are all sons of God through faith in Christ Jesus. For as many of you as were baptized into Christ have put on Christ. There is neither Jew nor Greek, there is neither slave nor free, there is neither male nor female; for you are all one in Christ Jesus (Galatians 3:26-28, NKJV).*

Our personal level of comfort along racial lines cannot be a consideration if we are in Christ and if we are to be effective witnesses for Him to the world around us.

The Lack of Diversity at Home

Unfortunately, the unity God calls for is not always evident in His Church today.

Again, some of our disunity rests on ingrained racism and ethnicity. We evaluate people who are different from us by the standards of our own race or ethnicity, and we consider anyone who is different to be inferior. While, in the U.S., it is easiest to point to racism against blacks that stems from slavery, the black–white divide is not the only one that exists.

Perhaps we are thinking a little more highly of ourselves than we ought to think (Romans 12:3). That's an affront to God, as there is only One who sees and judges.

When we negatively view with distain any person, because his or her skin is black, brown, red, white, or yellow, we sin against the God who created us in these various forms and whose Word considers all believers one in Christ Jesus (Galatians 3:28).

On the other hand, not all the division among believers is racism-based; some of it happens because we're just lax—we don't push ourselves. *So, we rarely worship or fellowship across lines of race, ethnicity, or class—not because we have anything against others, but because we don't invest the time into reaching out and building those relationships.*

With a few exceptions, we tend to stay connected with churches, or even with other believers in multicultural churches, who look like us and who share our general backgrounds. We do this because it's comfortable … and it's easy.

Whether because of racism or comfort, when we exclude ourselves from others along racial lines, we miss the tremendous opportunity to be a part of His beautiful diverse army flowing as one, as they champion the cause of Christ and worship Him.

Back on Track

The conclusion: We're off-track.

The question: What can we do to fix what's broken?

A look in the mirror certainly would help. If we believe that the body of Christ should be divided along racial lines, and should remain that way, we must question ourselves about the veracity of our faith and whether we truly are born of God. We are told in Scripture that we are to love one another because love comes from God who is love. And, if we are not showing love, then maybe we don't really know God (1 John 4:7-8). In another passage, John notes:

> *Anyone who claims to be in the light but hates a brother or sister is still in the darkness. Anyone who loves their brother and sister lives in the light, and there is nothing in them to make them stumble. But anyone who hates a brother or sister is in the darkness and walks around in the darkness. They do not know where they are going, because the darkness has blinded them (1 John 2:9-11, NIV).*

Although, many of us have read, heard, or even taught these passages, diversity remains one of the most challenging issues facing the Church today. *And, if our lack of diversity is based on a feeling of dislike and dishonor for those who are different, then that is a heart condition that we each must confront.* Are we willing to love like Jesus? Will we allow the grace that we've been given to operate in our lives so that we can extend a hand to those who may not look like us? Will we strive for unity in the Church? Will we ask the Holy Spirit to help us transcend our fears and embrace all parts of His body with love and acceptance?

If we want to please God, we must admit that racism is not of God; it is sin, and we must repent. It is an evil, manufactured by Satan to bring about division in the body of Christ. By buying into racism, we obscure the image of Christ's Church and hinder its ability to advance the kingdom.

For those of us who hold no ill-will, but who just don't seem to get around to engaging with believers from different backgrounds, we often do not realize it, we are missing an opportunity to show the world what the love of Christ looks like as we put diversity into practice. The Apostle Paul encouraged, "as we have opportunity, let us do good to all people, especially to those who belong to the family of believers" (Galatians 6:10, *NIV*).

Furthermore, if we are of Christ, in addition to practicing diversity and inclusion for ourselves, we must not be silent on issues related to racism and injustice in the world around us. We should be the first to speak out for acceptance and love for every race.

When Christ returns, He is coming back for a Church representing every nation. Revelation 7:9 (*NKJV*) tells us that John saw seated around the throne of God a vast crowd beyond man's power to number. They represented "every nation, tribe, people and language". Jesus taught us to pray for God's kingdom on earth to mirror the kingdom of heaven (Matthew 6:10). Well, if God has worship from a diverse body in heaven, that also is the way we should strive to make our worship on earth.

Finally, we must understand that Christ's gift of grace is available to everyone who calls on His name; it is not reserved for one group over another.

By grace, through faith in Him alone, are we saved, made members of His body, and gain the right to become His children (John 1:12). There is no partiality and prejudice with God (Romans 2:11).

Unless we, as the Church, change our perspective on this issue, the world will never change. As the Church of Jesus Christ, we are God's answer to racism and racial apathy. We are to show the world what the love of Christ looks like in action. Jesus said, "A new command I give you: Love one another. As I have loved you, so you must love one another. By this everyone will know that you are my disciples, if you love one another" (John 13: 34-35, NIV).

As believers when we show Christ's love, we can become an indomitable force in this world, tearing down the walls of racism and promoting the culture of God's kingdom.

Chapter 8

Fear vs. Boldness in Proclaiming the Gospel (Hindrance #6)

Boldness is the biblical way God wants the Gospel given. We are not to develop our own methods based on personality or passion. We are to open our mouths and unapologetically testify to the saving power of Jesus Christ. Is it possible that the commonly reported frustrations in personal evangelism and our epidemic failure to evangelize at all [are] rooted in our failure to embrace the biblical method of boldness?

~James McDonald

What does fear, and boldness have to do with advancing the Kingdom of God and proclaiming the gospel of Jesus Christ? Fear can paralyze our efforts, on the other hand, boldness makes us courageous and empowers us to speak and do what is necessary. However, without a doubt, fear might be the greatest impediment to believers' efforts to proclaim the gospel of Jesus Christ, share our testimonies and the most difficult spirits to overcome.

All of us fear something at some time. That's natural. But what is your fear holding you back from doing? Is that fear paralyzing? Does it keep you from fulfilling your dreams and doing God's will?

Fear may manifest in different forms and can be debilitating. When fear is debilitating; it takes our emotions, sense, and actions captive. This type of fear comes directly from Satan. It is having been his weapon against man since the beginning of time, and he continues to use it to defeat us and impede our mission as Christians.

This fear steals peace, feeds worry, and induces failure. And, when it arises in connection with our Great Commission charge, it causes us to feel inadequate, which strips us of boldness and hinders our ability to share the good news with others.

Boldness in the Bible

Throughout the Bible, God deals with fear among His people. It seems as if, on more than one occasion, God allows His people to get into situations beyond their control. Yet, each time such a scenario played out, God's words of reassurance and comfort followed: *Do not fear.*

There are too many references to list them all. However, we see Old Testament examples such as God's message to Moses while in the wilderness. Joshua received similar encouragement to be strong and courageous as the new leader of the people (Deuteronomy 31:7-8; Joshua 1:1-9). David also faced fear while in and out of battle, yet we have his reminders to himself that fear was unnecessary because God was with him (Psalm 23:4-5, 27:1-3).

New Testament figures also were encouraged not to fear as they were about to take on great works for God. The angel of the Lord told both Joseph and Mary not to be afraid as they walked through the events leading up to Jesus' birth (Matthew 1:20; Luke 1:30). Jesus instructed His disciples against fear repeatedly (Matthew 10:26-28, 14:27; Luke 5:10, 12:7; John 14:27). When Paul was about to minister to the people in Corinth, the Lord came to him in a vision and told him not to be afraid to speak up (Acts 18:9). Paul also later was encouraged not to be afraid before he was to appear before Caesar (Acts 27:23-26). Timothy was reminded that God didn't give him a spirit of fear, but one of power, love, and a sound mind (2 Timothy 1:7).

With just these few examples, we see an unmistakable message: *Fear does not come from God. To the contrary, He is ready and willing to strengthen us, to make us bold and courageous to do any work He has called us to do.*

Boldness to Carry Out the Great Commission

For what we have been called to do we need boldness. We have been called to carry out the Great Commission (Matthew 28:19-20). We are to go, make disciples, baptize people, and teach them how to live as Christ-Like lives. Operating in fear, holds us back from achieving this. It takes faith to give us the boldness to complete this assignment. *Faith is complete trust and confidence, in God. It is our reliance on the Spirit of God to give us power to be bold and effective witnesses. Faith and fear ... trust and doubt ... They cannot operate at the same time. In fact, when you think about it, fear is the opposite of faith.*

> *If you don't know what you're doing, pray to the Father. He loves to help. You'll get His help and won't be condescended to when you ask for it. Ask boldly, believingly, without a second thought. People who 'worry their prayers' are like wind-whipped waves. Don't think you're going to get anything from the Master that way, adrift at sea, keeping all your options open (James 1:5-8, MSG).*

What, then, is to be our approach? We are to proceed in *faith with boldness!* The disciples serve as our models. They were bold witnesses–did not water down the message of the gospel but who instead spoke bravely, openly, and persuasively, proclaiming Jesus and His resurrection from the dead (Acts 2:14-39, 3:11-26, 4:8-13). They did not operate in fear; they demonstrated faith in God. They trusted that He would empower them, at times deliver them, and even usher them to heaven if they were to die for the cause of Christ. They personally walked with Christ and knew the power of His resurrection now residing in them.

Perhaps that's one of the reasons why the Church is hampered today.

Many of us do not have a personal walk with Jesus. It is difficult to speak boldly about a God with whom we only have an arms-length connection. For others, we are afraid to offend and so we soft peddle the gospel. We don't want to upset our friends, colleagues, or communities, and so we mildly present the gospel as simply *an alternative*—one among many. I must admit that I've been guilty of this myself.

If we are being honest, though, this is not what we have been asked to do. We are to proclaim the gospel—to show people the way, not a way. Making that statement requires boldness.

No, our goal is not to annoy people intentionally; after all, we want them to be drawn to Christ, which is hard to accomplish if we are contrary and unkind in the way we approach them. However, boldness does mean that we are to be sure and uncompromising in presenting the truth. Such confidence in the unwavering truth of the gospel will be an offense to some unbelievers, even though we know, and we desperately want *them* to know too, that Christ is the only path to salvation for man.

As you read the New Testament, you discover that boldness in sharing the kingdom message carried a price. Many were imprisoned. Many were persecuted. All the disciples were killed for the faith, except John, who was banished to the Isle of Patmos until his death. And, of course, Christ Himself was crucified for speaking the truth. Boldness requires that one not fear death, imprisonment, or other persecution, though.

Boldness means standing confident in what you believe based on the truth God has revealed. It didn't matter to the disciples if people got upset or continued to like them. These pillars of the faith, and countless others, understood what they were called to do and stepped up with boldness, ready to pay the price.

Back on Track

We return to the Church of today. *How do we overcome our fear?* How do we step forward with boldness to be modern-day disciples who carry the banner of Christ to the world?

It begins by pursuing an intimate relationship with Christ ourselves. On our own, we have no strength. On our own, we will be unnerved and unable to step out. But, with Christ, and by the aid of the Holy Spirit, fear will disappear.

We remember that we can do all things through Christ which strengthen us (Philippians 4:13). When we depend on God, fear will be replaced with the boldness needed for whatever task He calls us to do. An ever-growing relationship with the author and completer of our faith helps us to learn that we don't have to rely on our own natural abilities as we witness. Instead, if God calls us to a work, He'll continue working in us, and through us, to accomplish it (Philippians 1:6).

Does a call for boldness mean that we will never experience fear? Not so; there will be times when the butterflies are uncorked. In those times, if we lean into God and pray, He will offer not only peace but also the right words to speak. He reminds us that we are not alone. We can rest on His strength and, as a result, we can testify boldly without worry about the reception. In fact, all we must do is be faithful in speaking the truth. As Paul said, "I planted the seed, Apollos watered it, but God has been making it grow. So, neither the one who plants nor the one who waters are anything, but only God, who makes things grow" (1 Corinthians 3:6-7, *NIV*). Some of the pressure is relieved when we remember that only God can transform a heart. He simply invites us to do the witnessing; we are to leave what comes next to Him.

How are we to address opposition when we step out boldly for Christ? In those times, it is essential that we remember that Christ not only foresaw resistance but experienced it Himself to the point of death on the cross.

If you find the godless world is hating you, remember it got its start hating me. If you lived on the world's terms, the world would love you as one of its own. But since I picked you to live on God's terms and no longer on the world's terms, the world is going to hate you.

★★★

I have told you all this so that trusting me, you will be unshakable and assured, deeply at peace. In this godless world you will continue to experience difficulties. But take heart! I've overcome the world (John 15:18-19, 16:33, MSG)

Although opposition is never easy to face, we have Jesus' model for handling it well and His promise that He's already been victorious over anything that may come our way. That makes the battle a bit easier to fight. Jesus also prayed protection for us against evil. He covers those who go into the world (John 17:14-19).

Finally, in the face of opposition, *we can tap into the power of our helper—the Holy Spirit—to inject us with the boldness we need.* When we resist trusting in ourselves, but instead rely on the inner witness of the Holy Spirit, He will strengthen us to speak in ways we never could on our own. He also makes us bold and effective witnesses, sharing the love of Christ, with speech that offers grace to the hearer, and God's mercy.

So, let me ask you. As a member of the Church of Christ, does fear separate you from living out your Great Commission assignment? If it does, please take some time for soul-searching.

- Have you been with Jesus lately?
- Have you truly surrendered so He can transform your life?
- Are you interested in becoming more like Jesus?

- Are you taking time regularly to build your faith through prayer and study?
- Have you asked the Holy Spirit for boldness to share the gospel?

May we have the boldness of the early church as presented in the book of Acts. May this prayer become yours as you move out in boldness to proclaim the gospel of Jesus Christ.

> *Dear Father,*
>   *Take care of the threats of the people who plot against Jesus and give Your servants fearless confidence in preaching Your message, as You stretch out Your hand to us in healings and miracles and wonders done in the name of Your holy servant Jesus.'*

While they were praying, it is recorded that the place where they were meeting trembled and shook. They were all filled with the Holy Spirit and continued to speak God's Word with fearless confidence (Acts 4:29-31, MSG).

May God honor our prayer, like theirs, and grant each of us boldness to speak His Word. And, may we, as the Church, have a powerful, and persuasive assurance—one that comes from God Himself—to proclaim the gospel everywhere we go.

Chapter 9

Missing Component: Making Disciples (Hindrance #8)

*Jesus-shaped spirituality hears Jesus say 'believe and repent,'
but the call that resonates most closely in the heart of a
disciple is 'follow me.' The command to follow requires that
we take a daily journey in the company of other students. It
demands that we be lifelong learners and that we commit to
constant growth in spiritual maturity. Discipleship is a call
to me, but it is a journey of 'we.'*

~Michael Spencer

The Great Commission is not only about sharing the gospel. At its core is the design to make disciples who also will make disciples.

However, for this disciple-making cycle to happen, church leaders, minsters, and other mature Christians must prepare men and women to be living epistles, or letters, to the world—men and women who walk and talk like Jesus. We must develop people who model Jesus' life so that others will be attracted to Him through us and will want to accept this way of life too.

What Does It Mean to Be a Disciple?

Unfortunately, the disciple-making concept is not well understood by most churches and even by some theologians. The word *disciple* comes from the Greek language. It refers to an individual student or apprentice, or to group of people who are the devoted followers of another. As defined in the Merriam-Webster Dictionary, a *disciple* is "one who accepts and assists in spreading the doctrines of another, such as a. Christianity … [or] b. a convinced adherent of a school or individual."

Most think that making disciples only means to evangelize the world by spreading the gospel. However, while disciple-making does start with a soul's conversion, as the definitions demonstrate, it is far more than that. It also is about teaching, training, and encouraging the believer to mature in the faith; it involves showing him or her how to live a righteous life, like Jesus did while He was here on earth.

Reaching unbelievers with the gospel has a purpose that far exceeds just filling the pews of our churches. Making disciples means that we help believers understand *that discipleship is a life-long process.* We must help them to take hold of the fact that they have been set aside to be holy and dedicated to the Lord, so they too may be used in this special work of discipleship. As ministers, we are to treat our church members as students and apprentices who also are being shaped to model the life of Jesus.

Jesus: The Model Disciple Maker

Jesus provided the model for disciple making. He had students; yet, He did not operate a formal school or program. Instead, in three short years, He taught His disciples and equipped them with what He had learned from the Father to live a righteous life. This small group spent time with Jesus, knew Him intimately, grew in grace daily, and followed in His footsteps in carrying the gospel to the world.

At the Heart of Disciple Making

Jesus established the discipleship model—belief and then commitment.

Salvation begins the process. Jesus said to Nicodemus: Unless one is born again, he cannot see the kingdom of God" (John 3:3, NKJV). Being born again—recognizing that Jesus is God's Son, believing that He is the only path to the Father, and receiving His gift of salvation—is the first step to discipleship. For, if one does not know Him, how can he or she be an effective witness of Him?

On the road to discipleship, the journey starts with learning about Christ's character and nature and then to shaping our character and nature to His. Luke recorded Jesus as saying that, "[a] disciple is not above his teacher, but everyone who is perfectly trained will be like his teacher" (Luke 6:40, *NKJV*). Our goal, in becoming disciples, is to be like Jesus, our teacher.

Though we cannot be with Christ in the natural, as some members of the early Church were, we still have the privilege of getting to know Him through the His Word, through the Holy Spirit who indwells us, and through people of God who teach and mentor us.

Jesus demonstrated this principle to His disciples on many occasions, but one that comes to mind is referenced by John.

> *When He had finished washing their feet, He put on His clothes and returned to His place. 'Do you understand what I have done for you?' He asked them. 'You call Me 'Teacher' and 'Lord', and rightly so, for that is what I am. Now that I, your Lord and Teacher, have washed your feet, you also should wash one another's feet. I have set you an example that you should do as I have done for you. Very truly I tell you, no servant is greater than his master, nor is a messenger greater than the one who sent him. Now that you know these things, you will be blessed if you do them (John 13:12-17, NIV).*

Again, Jesus was talking directly to the disciples who were there with Him that day; however, His message extends to us as well. As imitators of Christ, we are to do what He did and what He tells us to do.

Back on Track

Each of us who calls Christ our Savior now has two roles. We must continue to be discipled, and we are to go out and make disciples.

Growing as a Disciple of Christ

Being continually trained as a disciple and seeking to live as a disciple are not always easy tasks. Discipleship, however, is a choice. It is a choice that Jesus also made while on earth. As a man, He was discipled by the Father.

> *Most assuredly, I say to you, the Son can do nothing of Himself, but what He sees the Father do; for whatever He does, the Son also does in like manner. For the Father loves the Son and shows Him all things that He Himself does; and He will show Him greater works than these, that you may marvel (John 5:19-20, NKJV).*

So, if we are to follow in Christ's footsteps, we must be teachable. Some of us are more receptive to teaching when we are new in the faith; yet, Jesus' own life shows us that, all along one's journey, true disciples are students. We must be willing to deny self, dispose of our selfish and prideful ways, and choose to follow God's instructions about how to live out our lives. Jesus said,

"*Whoever wants to be My disciple must deny themselves and take up their cross daily and follow [Me" (Luke 9:23, NIV). Following Christ may mean releasing the grip on family members or possessions that divert our attention from God and the path He has set us on as disciples (Luke 14: 26-27).*

Denying ourselves may mean letting go of personal or church agendas, especially those that don't line up with His. In other words, whether facing something harmful or a call to surrender something, good or bad, God calls us to be willing to let go and follow His lead.

And, when we do, Jesus promises that we will be rewarded for any losses we suffer. He said that those who leave friends, family, houses, and so on, for His sake, will receive a hundred-fold more in life and in eternity than what was lost (Mark 10:28-30).

What do we gain? Our ongoing discipleship journey allows us to know God and grow in Him. As we do, we recognize that it is all about His mission. As we abide and experience the Holy Spirit, we discover that it is only through Him that we can have the life that He desires for us. Scripture tell us that:

> *God knew what He was doing from the very beginning. He decided from the outset to shape the lives of those who love Him along the same lines as the life of His Son. The Son stands first in the line of humanity He restored. We see the original and intended shape of our lives there in Him. After God made that decision of what His children should be like, He followed it up by calling people by name. After He called them by name, He set them on a solid basis with Himself. And then, after getting them established, He stayed with them to the end, gloriously completing what He had begun (Romans 8:29-30, MSG).*

Everyone that is born of His Spirit has been called to live like Him. *Salvation gets us into the kingdom of God; discipleship conforms us to Christ's image.*

Planting Discipleship Seeds in Others

People tend to think that carrying the word is the exclusive responsibility of those in full-time ministry, but that is not so. Every one of us has a Great Commission charge, and each of us is to be both on the lookout for opportunities to share with others and ready to step forward when sharing occasions arise.

On the other hand, our assignment with respect to others does not stop with evangelism. If salvation were the whole story, then new believers would be stunted spiritually and remain babies. *Unfortunately, many—even long-time believers—have not progressed beyond spiritual infancy or the teenaged phase, often because they are not surrounded by spiritually mature believers or mature believers who are committed to aiding in their spiritual development. With that as the church environment, it's no wonder why we have so many who are weak in their faith, impotent, and lacking a deep commitment to Christ.*

As the Apostle Paul wrote, *"When I was a child, I spoke as a child, I understood as a child, I thought as a child; but when I became a man, I put away childish things" (1 Corinthians 13:11, NKJV).* Infancy is a natural stage of development. Babies need milk—the easily digestible versions of the Word of God—so that they may grow in that stage. Similarly, children and teens in the faith also need the Word along with caring adults to guide their steps and to help them mature. *But, the unmistakable goal is maturity.* God's intent never is to have people remain as young children; the design is to help us become whole, strong men and women—always learning, but now able to guide others in truth and authority because we ourselves are well connected to Christ. For this type of maturity to occur within the body, new believers need seasoned mentors to come alongside to instruct and to model righteous living.

Jesus was a mentor, and He set the example for us to follow. Jesus came alongside His disciples, developed an intimate relationship with them, answered their questions, responded to their needs, and challenged them.

The disciples were Jesus's students and His apprentices for three years. As they followed Him, their lives were transformed. Jesus established a pattern for relationship building and discipleship—one that we should follow. Making disciples is not an overnight experience nor is it always an easy assignment. Discipleship is a process that begins with building relationship and requires an investment of time. An assembly-line mentality will not be effective. We must be willing to invite the Spirit to point us to people who are ready for the discipleship journey, and then follow His lead. We must be willing to come alongside those who have been identified, wherever they find themselves on their faith journey, so that we can teach them how to follow Christ and how to embrace the lifestyle that He has outlined. And, we must be willing to stay connected with them until maturity in Christ is visible in their lives.

When we are willing to join God in the process, whether we plant or water, we play a significant role in making disciples. Completing the transformative work in people's lives does not rest with us; only the Holy Spirit can change a life and bring about growth (1 Corinthians 3:5-8). Yet, Jesus invites us to participate. He wants us to partner with Him in making new, as well as, equipping existing disciples who will go out and do likewise.

So, are you ready? Are you willing to go forth in the power of the Holy Spirit, to tell others about Jesus, and to teach them how to live sanctified lives? *You may be the only Jesus that they see, the only Bible that they read and the only one to tell them about Christ's love for them.*

Chapter 10
Satan: The Author of Division (Hindrance #9)

It is important to note that though most of the attack on believers seems to come through humans, we must see the devil as the ultimate force behind it all. It's easy to get frustrated and even resentful toward others who oppose the cause of Christ, but they must not be the primary cause or the primary enemy. People are only prisoners of war being used like puppets in the hands of Satan. People are to be loved as deceived as they may be. They are the mission field that needs to be set free from their bondage as they exist entombed in their false beliefs. ★★★ Our enemy is the devil himself. We struggle not against flesh and blood (Ephesians 6:12).
~Randy Smith

Whether we acknowledge or not, we are in spiritual warfare. Our enemy is Satan, and he utilizes the full resources of his kingdom of darkness at every possible turn.

Who Opposes Us?

If the Church of Christ is to live victoriously and fulfill the Great Commission, it is necessary for us to understand our enemy, and our opposition. *Our opposition is Satan—a created being.* He originally served as God's chief worshipper, leading the angelic choir in praise to the Almighty. However, at some point along the way, his focus changed; he wanted the praise for himself rather than giving it to God. As recounted in the Book of Isaiah:

> *How you are fallen from heaven,*
> *O Lucifer son of the morning!*
> *How you are cut down to the ground,*
> *You who weakened the nations!*
> *For you have said in your heart:*
> *'I will ascend into heaven,*
> *I will exalt my throne above the stars of God;*
> *I will also sit on the mount of the congregation*
> *On the farthest sides of the north;*
> *I will ascend above the heights of the clouds,*
> *I will be like the Most- High (Isaiah 14:12-14, NKJV).*

His rebellion, and desire essentially to take God's place led to him being banished from heaven and sent to earth (Revelation 12:7-9). In the process, he convinced a third of the angels to join his crusade against God. Though no longer in heaven, His plan did not change. We see evidence of Satan throughout the Bible attempting to sway people away from God and to himself (Genesis 3:1-6; 1 Chronicles 21:1; Job 1:6-12; Matthew 4:1-11; Mark 8:33; John 13:27; Acts 5:3; 1 Timothy 1:20).

Scripture tells us that Satan sinned from the outset (1 John 3:8) and that he is alive and active in the earth even now. As believers and growing disciples, we must realize him as the chief deceiver.

Jesus referred to him as "a murderer from the beginning, not holding to the truth, for there is no truth in him. When he lies, he speaks his native language, for he is a liar and the father of lies" (John 8:44, *NIV*). Jesus also warned us that he is thief, who "comes only to steal and kill and destroy" (John 10:10, *NIV*). What we sometimes miss, though, is that Satan is already a defeated enemy. His end has been foretold, and it was set in motion by Christ's death and resurrection (John 12:31, 16:11). Not only did Christ's victory over death take away the sting that Satan believed he had struck with the crucifixion, it also opened a pathway to eternal life for anybody who would choose Christ (1 Corinthians 15:54-57). Though still struggling to wreak havoc, his end is clearly foreseen. In the Book of Revelation, his outcome is reported *"The devil, who deceived them, was cast into the lake of fire and brimstone where the beast and the false prophet are. And they will be tormented day and night forever and ever"* (Revelation 20:10, NKJV).

The Fight Today

So, the body of Christ—the Church—has an enemy. Though ultimately defeated, he is not going down without a fight.

Satan in some way affects every area of life: economy, family, church, political and governmental systems, and entertainment to name a few. Satan is casing us, studying us, and pursuing us to control our minds— whispering evil thoughts into our ears, thoughts of murder; of suicide; of alcohol, drugs, sex, gambling, gaming, and other abuses; of doubt, fear, unbelief, shame, humiliation, and condemnation. He uses any means necessary to pollute the body of Christ and render us useless. His goal is to wear us out and prevent us from carrying on our Great Commission charge concerning the saving of souls and cultivating a body of strong, maturing saints of God. *Why?* He knows that, if we are mired down in our own mess, or if our lives and walk are compromised, we become ineffective in bringing forth the good news; we become a disadvantage to God in proclaiming the coming of His kingdom.

So how is it that we, the Church of Christ, have gotten caught unaware? I see three reasons why we have been deceived and disabled.

Diligence

First, we have not been diligent. Scripture makes many references to being on watch (Judges 7:19; 2 Samuel 13:34; 2 Chronicles 23:6;

Nehemiah 4:9; Matthew 24:42-44; Mark 13:34; 1 Corinthians 16:13; 2 Timothy 4:5). Earlier we talked about the concept of watchmen—people who were positioned to stand guard, with eyes wide open, against possible invasion and harm.

Our pastors and ministers certainly should be one line of watch for us as a body; however, all of us should have open eyes for what may come our way. And, to be honest, we all have failed.

Though some of the instruments Satan uses today may be different than in the past, his strategies, character, and tactics are largely the same as they have been since the beginning. We should be on the lookout for outright lies, for instances when biblically based teaching is subtly replaced by humanism and generic spirituality, or anything that draw us away from righteousness, or ultimately lead to our demise and destruction. Yes, Satan engages in subtle tactics to undermine the church and its ministers daily. We have not kept watch. We have gotten lax and have begun to accept everything that sounds good as being of God, but it's just not so. Our lack of diligence has left us vulnerable to Satan and his false prophets, who cleverly integrates the world's culture into church activities and sermons (2 Corinthians 11:13-15).

Drifted

We have drifted. Our failure to remain close to God has contributed to our powerlessness. Jesus called Himself the true (or the good) shepherd (John 10:1-30). He and His sheep are intimately connected. He knows His sheep, and His sheep know Him. His sheep know His voice and do not respond to the voice of a strangers. He stayed with His sheep as they remained in His care. This same type of relationship is desired of us. Spending time in communion with God is the beginning of developing and intimate relationship with God. As Jesus said, "Abide in Me, and I in you. As the branch cannot bear fruit of itself, unless it abides in the vine, neither can you, unless you abide in Me" *(John 15:4, NKJV).*

But, if we fail to invest time into building a relationship with God, it's no wonder that, like seeds that are tossed by the wayside, Satan can take what we do learn and twist it or wipe it quickly away.

Without abiding in Him and His Word, we do not develop soil rich enough to ward off the attacks of the enemy (Mark 4:1-20). In John 8:44 (NIV), we read that Jesus called Satan "the father of lies". And, how do we combat lies? We abide in Christ and His Words.

Abiding is more than stopping by occasionally for a visit; abiding is lingering, soaking Him in, and savoring the relationship. Abiding is what we see from Martha's sister, Mary, in Luke 10:39. Abiding is what Jesus encouraged the disciples to do, as He likened Himself to the vine and them to the branches, noting that without that constant connection, and the exchange that happens during it, they would be fruitless (John 15:1-8).

To abide, we must resist the spirit of apathy for God and His Word that Satan tries to infuse into our lives. For, without that time abiding in our Creator, we will continue to wander deceived, fearful, self-absorbed, disobedient, prideful, confused, and ignorant of our identity in Christ and the authority that comes along with it (1 John 2:24; John 15:7). Without time abiding with Him, we do not learn to walk as Christ walked (1 John 2:6). When we fail to abide, we accomplish little of God's plan for us because, as Jesus explicitly said, "Without Me you can do nothing" (John 15:5, *NKJV*). And *nothing* is exactly what Satan wants us to do.

Preparedness

Many of us simply are unprepared to fight. Either we are clueless that a battle is even waging, or we are fighting with the wrong weapons.

Once we become aware of Satan's presence and his attacks against us, we are foolish if we try to fight on our own. Yet, many of us do just that. We attempt to fight with our strong wills, or our own strategies, or what we think, or phrases we've heard others say. But we're fighting all wrong. The Bible tells us that, to withstand the schemes of the evil one, we must recognize what we're dealing with and fight using the tools that God has provided.

> *For our struggle is not against flesh and blood, but against the rulers, against the authorities, against the powers of this dark world and against the spiritual forces of evil in the heavenly realms. Therefore, put on the full armor of God, so that when the day of evil comes, you may be able to stand your ground, and after you have done everything, to stand. Stand firm then, with the belt of truth buckled around your waist, with the breastplate of righteousness in place, and with your feet fitted with the readiness that comes from the gospel of peace. In addition to all this, take up the shield of faith, with which you can extinguish the flaming arrows from the evil one. Take the helmet of salvation and the sword of the Spirit, which is the Word of God (Ephesians 6:10-17, NIV).*

Because our fight is not against a physical enemy, we can't use physical or natural means to battle back. We can't fight these battles exclusively in the courts, or at the polls, or using any other human means. Because this war is against powers that are spiritual, the underlying battle method likewise must be spiritual in nature. We have been given spiritual weapons by God that will enable us to stand and to be victorious over Satan.

We are to cloak ourselves from head-to-toe in the armor of God so that we can be protected against Satan's schemes. And, in those instances when we must go on the offensive, we are to do exactly what Christ did when Satan sought to tempt Him in the wilderness; we are to use the sword of the Spirit, which is the Word of God (Matthew 4:1-11). When we wield this sword, Satan will depart, as he did with Jesus, because he cannot fight the Word when it is used with precision and assurance. As Jesus promised, when we move forward in His authority—in the power and might of the Word that became flesh and dwelt among us—nothing ultimately can hurt us (Luke 10:19; John1:1-2, 14).

To engage in a spiritual battle, we must be prepared. We must be knowledgeable of the tools that we have at our disposal and know how to use them. God has given us a full set of armor, to protect us in battle, the shield of faith, the sword of the Spirit, the Word of God. We have all the tools that we need to stand against the enemy from a position of victory. Christ has defeated the Devil and we are more than conquerors through Him (Romans 8:37).

Back on Track

Satan has a mission, and that mission is to wear us out—to exhaust, hurt, crush, damage, and consume us. He wants either to so distract us, or to make us so weak internally and/or to those around us, that our Great Commission calling goes by the wayside.

So, what do we do?

A good start is to refocus on the very areas in which we tend to fall short.

We must raise our level of awareness. We must be on guard, especially related to the avenues that Satan uses to trip us up as individuals and as a body.

Think about it. In our churches, we seldom hear messages or receive instruction about Satan's existence or how he seeks to impede believers. *However, when we ignore him, we leave ourselves open to his attacks.* When we fail to warn others, especially those whom we are discipling, we fail to ready them for the battle that they are already in ... whether they know it or not.

Now, do not misunderstand. We are not to put all our focus on the evil one and take our eyes off Jesus. That's an unproductive tactic.

On the other hand, it is important to be on guard, "sober, vigilant; because [our] adversary the devil walks about like a roaring lion, seeking whom he may devour" (1 Peter 5:8, *NKJV*). When we are diligent, close, and prepared for battle, we remember that we are His sheep, and we belong to God (Psalm 100:3). With confidence in who we are and whose we are, we come to realize that the battle is not ours; it's the Lord's (2 Chronicles 20:15). Because we belong to God, we need not fear. We know that the victory already has been won. He will come and save us (Isaiah 35:4). Even if we suffer for what is right, we needn't fear because we know that He will heal and restore us (1 Peter 3:14).

No devil, government, person, or power is greater than the Spirit of God, who is within us (1 John 4:4).

So, we have a Great Commission assignment to complete. We also have an enemy who is poised to interfere with our task at every turn. *We must remember that, Christ refused to allow the forces of hell to thwart the building of His Church (Matthew 16:18).* If we are to play our part in fulfilling the His Great Commission plan, we too must make our minds up that we cannot allow anyone to deter us from our calling.

Chapter 11

Without Love (Hindrance 9)

In biblical thinking, genuine love exists only when good works are done in a context where God rather than the doer gets the credit.

~Daniel Fuller

Some Christians mistakenly believe that gathering at church is our exclusive way of worshipping God. Corporate worship certainly has its place, but it is only a part of what we have been called to do. Others believe that, by exercising spiritual gifts, they are acting out their faith. While the Spirit deposits at least one gift in each believer for us to use, even when we are functioning in our giftedness, this still is not all we are called to do. Some think that, if they do good works, such as outreach to the needy, they are fulfilling God's command. Again, that is indeed a noble deed, but the truth is that it does not convey the full extent of our calling either.

Though all of these and others are important functions for us as members of the body of Christ, none of these good things surpasses the best thing—love. No matter what our spiritual gifting may be, and no matter how many good works we may do, none of it amounts to much if it is done without God's love working in and through us.

It may be that we do not understand how love works in our mission. We do not understand that even if we may go through the motions of evangelism or disciple-making, if we are doing this this without sharing love, Christ's message is presented incomplete. Everything that we do is because of the love of Christ and God's love for mankind. His love is our motivating force.

The Importance of Love

Perhaps the most well-known instruction on love was written by the Apostle Paul.

> If I speak with human eloquence and angelic ecstasy but don't love, I'm nothing but the creaking of a rusty gate.
>
> If I speak God's Word with power, revealing all His mysteries and making everything plain as day, and if I have faith that says to a mountain, 'Jump,' and it jumps, but I don't love, I'm nothing.
>
> If I give everything I own to the poor and even go to the stake to be burned as a martyr, but I don't love, I've gotten nowhere. So, no matter what I say, what I believe, and what I do, I'm bankrupt without love (1 Corinthians 13:1-7, MSG).

There is absolutely no force on earth as powerful as love. It is the only one thing that can bring about unity in the Church, eradicate hate, and overcome the tactics of the enemy that contribute to the defeat in our lives. It can transcend everything and anything. It is the ultimate answer to any problem we face personally or in the world around us. Love—God's love— conquers all. And, I mean all.

God's Love at Work for, in, and through Us

It is possible for us to know what love is in human terms without knowing what love is in heavenly terms. As humans, we love when we feel a deep affection for another person or thing. God's brand of love —His agape love— encompasses that and so much more. The Bible tells us that:

Love never gives up.
Love cares more for others than for self.
Love doesn't want what it doesn't have.
Love doesn't strut,
Doesn't have a swelled head,
Doesn't force itself on others,
Isn't always 'me first,'
Doesn't fly off the handle,
Doesn't keep score of the sins of others,
Doesn't revel when others grovel,
Takes pleasure in the flowering of truth,
Puts up with anything,
Trusts God always,
Always looks for the best,
Never looks back,
But keeps going to the end
(1 Corinthians 13:4-7, *MSG*).

This kind of love—God's kind of love— has no limits.

God's Love for Us

Love like this isn't just nice words on a page; it's active. God demonstrated His love for us. We know that "this is how much God loved the world: He gave His Son, His one and only Son. And therefore: so that no one need be destroyed; by believing in Him, anyone can have a whole and lasting life" (John 3:16, MSG). *While we were still sinners, Christ died for us" (Romans 5:8, NIV).* God gave His very best, and His dearest, so that we—very messed-up people—could become His children (Romans 8:14-17).

It is impossible for any of us to carry out the Great Commission if we have not first experienced God's love. We may attempt to lead others to Christ, and we may show others how to live righteously, but without God's true love residing within us, it really does become nothing more than a "sounding brass or a clanging cymbal", as one version of 1 Corinthians 13:1 puts it. *We cannot authentically pass on to someone else something we have not felt for ourselves.*

If we are unable to love others regardless of who they are or where they come from, we must do as Apostle Paul suggested *"Examine yourself to see whether you are in the faith; test yourself" (2 Corinthians 13:5, NIV).* Ask yourself whether you actually have taken the step of faith to accept Jesus as your Savior and Lord and receive His life-changing gift of love. If you have not, it's not too late! Please don't allow pride to stand in the way of you experiencing God's unmatched love and being ushered into eternal life in the presence of God Almighty.

God's Love in Us

Jesus let us know the depth of His love for us. He said. *"As the Father has loved Me, so have I loved you. Now remain in My love" (John 15:9, NIV).* Psalm 23 offers another example. There we see God's love likened to that of a shepherd for the sheep. He guides us to rest when we're tired, leads us to easily accessible water, helps us to regain our strength, protects us from actual or threatened of harm, shows our enemies that we are favored and under His care, and offers us a place with Him now and for eternity.

Scripture also reveals that God loves His children so much that He's working in us continually to sanctify and shape us into Christ's image (Romans 8:28-29; 1 Corinthians 6:11). Despite all of this, sometimes we become unnerved and wonder whether God's love is always available to us, but He loves us so much that He wants us to be secure and assured of our position in Him. *The Bible tells us that we are bound to God forever by His Love and that absolutely nothing can ever separate us from Him (Romans 8:35-39).*

When we remember just how far God's love has brought us, we should be inspired to want nothing less than to do what we can to advance the Great Commission.

We see in Romans 5:8 that, when we were still in our pitiful, sinful state, God allowed Jesus to die for us.

As Tony Evans says in connection with grace, we don't deserve what God has done for us, and we can never repay Him for it. When we really come to grips with that truth about how God deals with us, how can we help but love Him?

Jesus was eager to pass His love on to the disciples and invited them to abide in His love (John 15:9). He wanted them to know deep down that they were loved, and He wants the same for us. He doesn't offer us a surface type of love but the security that His love is forever. As we experience His love, we begin to know His love and become more comfortable about sharing His love with others.

God's Love through Us

While on earth, Jesus not only instructed His disciples about loving others, He showed them up close how that looked. In His teaching, He reminded them of the law:

"'You shall love the Lord your God with all of your heart, with all your soul, and with all your mind.' This is the first and great commandment. And the second is like it: 'You shall love your neighbor, as yourself'" (Matthew 22:38-39, NKJV).

Jesus also demonstrated. We see reports of love demonstrated throughout the Gospels, such as the love that took Jesus to dinner at the house of Zacchaeus, the tax collector (Luke 19:1-10); or the love that was shown in His refusal to banish the children who were brought to Him (Luke 18:15-17); or that caused Him to weep as He saw His dear friends Martha and Mary's heartbreak over the death of their brother Lazarus (John 11:1-37). Jesus' modeled how we are to express God's love to the people around us. He loved people and, in so doing, pointed them to the Father—His source of love. And, He wanted us to do likewise.

"A new commandment I give to you, that you love one another; as I have loved you, that you also love one another. By this all will know that you are

My disciples, if you have love for one another" (John 13:34-35, NKJV). *You see, in each of us, this love resides, and God intends for us to share it.*

When love prevails in the body of Christ, the people of the world get to see what real love looks like. As important as it is for us to love our neighbors outside of the church walls, it is equally important to show the world how well we love one another within the household of faith (Galatians 6:10).

When they see us love one another in the faith, they get a glimpse of how God's love binds people together regardless of age, race, gender, or social economic backgrounds. They get a chance to see how God's love unifies. This type of love—love that makes no earthly sense—is what distinguishes us as children of God (Matthew 5:43-48).

Living a life of love, as Christ would, is achievable only when we depend on the power of the Holy Spirit to build our faith and keep us firmly established in God's love (Jude 20-21). As we walk in Christ's love, His grace sustains us, and He gives us the necessary attitude and action steps to love others. As unbelievers come to understand that the Love of God not like natural love; fleeting or unstable but His love is constant and matchless.

Back on Track

So, if the Church is to truly to take on the Great Commission charge, we must understand that there is no other way to fulfill the Great Commission, except living this life of love. He calls us to a mission of love, one in which He redeems mankind unto Himself, from every, tribe, nation and language; through power of our voice, actions and lifestyle.

There no power greater than the Father and the Son's love for us. No other love can bring salvation, healing, eradicate hatred, selfishness, and division. Evil cannot penetrate or destroy God's love-His love is everlasting. What joy we discover when we allow His love to rule and be released through us to others.

Chapter 12
Missing Dynamic-Worship (Hindrance 10)

Human beings by their very nature are worshipers. Worship is not something we do; it defines who we are. You cannot divide human beings into those who worship and those who don't. Everybody worships; it's just a matter of what, or whom, we serve."

Paul David Tripp

I hear the Father and the Voice of our Lord, saying. *"If but My People who are Called by My Name would worship Me, I'd cause heaven to touch earth, the earth would be filled with my Glory.*

It seems as if people are worshipping anything and everything rather than God; money, success, materialism, jobs, political officials and parties, entertainers, sports, husbands, children, causes, other little gods and themselves. No matter where you go throughout the world we find people worshipping something or someone; statues, animals, mother earth and even water. If we are truthful, we will discover that someone or something is the object of our affection and focus rather than God. Often, we do not realize that we have substituted worship of God for things and people, simply, because most of us have no concept of what worship is, and what it looks like.

Most associate worship with what happens in church on Sunday mornings when we participate in singing praise and worship songs. But true worship is more than a church experience or style of music.

Worship is more than a song. John Piper, author and theologian said this. *True worship is valuing or treasuring God above all things even our desires."*

Today, it is one of the missing dynamics in most believers' lives. Placing God above all else, seems to be challenging since there all so many things and distractions pulling at our heart strings. More and more, we find our affections turning to things and people rather than God. These things occupy the place in our heart that has been created for the worship of God. As time pass, we feel disconnected from the Spirit of God because nothing can fill that place in our hearts that has been created and set apart for the worshipping Him. *Worship is about Who He is, who we are and how we respond.* It is about having a heart, thirst and appetite for worship of Him that can only be filled by Himself.

Pastor, Bill Johnson, of Bethel Church made this profound statement about worship. He said. *"The heart to seek God is birthed in us by God Himself. Like all desires, it is not something that can be legislated or forced, but rather it grows within us as we become exposed to God's nature. He creates an appetite in us for Himself by lavishing us with the reality of His goodness—His irresistible glory. The realities of His goodness burn deeply into the hearts of all who simply take the time to behold Him".*

Throughout history and the bible, God makes it clear that He is the only one to be worshipped. While the Israelites were being delivered from the hands of the Egyptians, God said to them. *"You must worship no other gods, for the Lord, whose very name is Jealous. He is a God who is jealous about his relationship with you (Exodus 34:14)."* He further expounded on this when He instructed Moses to tell them this. *"You must not have any other god but me. You must not make for yourself an idol of any kind or an image of anything in the heavens or on the earth or in the sea. You must not bow down to them or worship them, for I, the Lord your God, am a jealous God who will not tolerate your affection for any other gods. I lay the sins of the parents upon their children; the entire family is affected—even children in the third and fourth generations of those who reject me. But I lavish unfailing love for a thousand generations on those who love me and obey my commands. (Exodus 20:3-6)".*

This is a reminder to us today, that our God is a jealous God, Who, desires and demands nothing less than a people who worships Him above everything.

You may ask why is worship so important to our Creator? There is a simple answer to this question. He is our Creator. There is no one greater than He or as powerful as He. For there is not anything or anyone that exist that He did not create. He alone is the almighty one, the all sufficient, the beginning and ending. To worship Him is not a consideration or option. It is a command from God, Himself. Only He is worthy to receive glory and honor and power (Rev 4:11). Worship is one of the channels that He uses to communicate with us and draw us into an intimate relationship with Him. His love for us is *irrevocable, indescribable and not be measured.* His greatness, value and worth cannot be appraised.

So now that we know all these things about our Lord, how do we really worship God? I've pondered the same question. Jesus answers this question when He meets with the Samaritan woman, who has come to draw water out of the well. When she approached the well, Jesus was there and asked her to give Him a drink. Since He was a Jew she was puzzled over Him asking her for a drink since Samaritans did not talk with Jews. In part because there was an ongoing argument between Jews and Samaritans over where people should worship. This woman entered into a discussion with Jesus, about where one should worship. She was confused as many of us are about what worship is and where it should take place. Jesus answered her and said. *"But the hour is coming, and is now here, when the true worshipers will worship the Father in spirit and truth, for the Father is seeking such people to worship him. God is Spirit and those who worship Him must worship Him in spirit and truth (John 4:21-24)"*

Just, what does this mean- *to worship God in Spirit and Truth*? Jesus was speaking prophetically about a future time when the Holy Spirit would indwell each believer. Well, that time is here. Through Jesus, each of us have the Holy Spirit abiding in us. We now are able to worship God in Spirit and Truth. God has given us Himself through

Jesus Christ and in the person of the Holy Spirit so that we can worship Him, authentically. There is literally nothing standing in the way of our worship of Him. We now have access to God through His indwelling Spirit and the Lord Jesus Christ. We can actively pursue a lifestyle of worship because we have been born of and filled with His Spirit. Without His Spirit we will never be true worshippers. He brings face to face with our Creator, Spirit to spirit.

The Holy Spirit also helps us present ourselves before the Lord, holy and acceptable. This is a reasonable response for all He has done for us and truly the way to worship Him. As we pour ourselves out as an offering to Him, in turn, He transforms us into true worshippers. Our natural is exchanged for the spiritual as we are changed from glory to glory.

Apostle Paul said this. *And so, dear brothers and sisters, I plead with you to give your bodies to God because of all he has done for you. Let them be a living and holy sacrifice—the kind he will find acceptable. This is truly the way to worship him (Romans 12:1-3 NIV).*

When I think of worship, there is no one in the Bible who worshipped God as David did. David possessed a heart of worship. He did not have the indwelling of the Holy Spirit as we do. But, we are told that the Spirit of Lord came upon him (1 Samuel 16:13) and enabled Him to worship God like any other. David was an unrestrained worshipper. He literally danced in the streets, nearly naked. He was not ashamed of worshipping God. He revered, honored, exalted, adored, glorified and praised our God. He knew that He could not live without God's presence in His life. His heart was fixed on God for God had been merciful and faithful to Him. He made God His priority and the object of His affection.

I challenge you today, to open your hearts to worship. Worship God with all of your being, mind, soul and strength. In your worship of Him, you will begin to see God in His glory and experience a bit of heaven touching earth. As you step into this lifestyle of worship, you will see miracles happen. Your life will be brought into alignment with His will and you will reflect Who He is in the world. Bondages will be broken, bodies will be healed, peace and joy will be restored and fill your hearts. Then you will begin to discover His worth, value, love, glorious majesty, supremacy, and authority.

I encourage you to make every effort to make God your daily priority. Don't be comfortable with just your usual Sunday worship experience. Release the worshipper – the Holy Spirit- within you. When the worshipper is released in you, you might want to dance like David danced.

Who knows what will happen when you begin living a life of worship, people may want to know about the God that you worship. Living a life of worship is not confined within the walls of the church, you must live it everywhere you go.

According to Judson Cornwall, *worship is written upon the heart of man by the hand of God and the two are inseparable. We have been given an eternal invitation to become God's instrument of worship. It is the highest calling and expression of our love for our Father.*

Remember, worship is more than the songs we sing but it also the Life that We Live!

Chapter 13

Called to Light up the World with the Light of Christ

Give light, and the darkness will disappear of itself.
~Desiderius Erasmus

Christ's vision is plain, and His mission has been declared. The Church has been called out of darkness and into the marvelous light to make an impact for God on the world. Jesus said it this way to His followers, according to The Message:

> *Let me tell you why you are here. You're here to be salt-seasoning that brings out the God-flavors of this earth. If you lose your saltiness, how will people taste godliness? You've lost your usefulness and will end up in the garbage.*
>
> *Here's another way to put it: You're here to be light, bringing out the God-colors in the world. God is not a secret to be kept. We're going public with this, as public as a city on a hill. If I make you light-bearers, you don't think I'm going to hide you under a bucket, do you? I'm putting you on a light stand. Now that I've put you there on a hilltop, on a light stand—shine! Keep open house; be generous with your lives. By opening to others, you'll prompt people to open with God, this generous Father in heaven (Matthew 5:13-16, MSG).*

We have been indwelled with God Himself—*the Light of the World*. Now, it's time to shine! We have all heard messages about being lights, but do we really know what it means to be an instrument that God can use to light up the world?

Discovering the Light

Light … it's the thing that makes sight possible. *Light* … it's the thing that erases darkness.

Light is vital to everything in life. It triggers many of the chemical and biological reactions that occur on earth. Humans need it to guide and enable us to go about our daily activities. Light helps us convey messages. Light powers our world.

Light did not just appear. God very intentionally created it. In fact, light was God's first creative work, manifesting His divine operation and dispelling chaos and darkness.

> *The earth was without form, and void; and darkness was on the face of the deep. And the Spirit of God was hovering over the face of the waters.*
>
> *Then God said, 'Let there be light'; and there was light. And God saw the light, that it was good; and God divided the light from the darkness. God called the light Day, and the darkness He called Night. So, the evening and the morning were the first day (Genesis 1:2-5, NKJV).*

Throughout the Bible, light represents God's divine presence. In the Old Testament, for instance, God went before the Israelites at night as a pillar of fire, giving them light and guiding their way through the wilderness (Exodus 13:21-22). David referred to the Lord as his "light" and "salvation", and because of that realization, he knew that he needn't be afraid (Psalm 27:1). The writer of another psalm noted that "Your word is a lamp to my feet and a light to my path" (Psalm 119:105, *NKJV*). Isaiah encouraged the people, "O house of Jacob, come and let us walk in the light of the Lord" (Isaiah 2:5, *NKJV*).

When we read the New Testament, though, writers specifically point to Jesus as being the Light. *John tells us that "in Him was life, and the life was the light of men. The light shines in the darkness, and the darkness has not overcome it" (John 1:4-5, NIV).* Matthew writes about Jesus' fulfillment of earlier prophesy: Luke records Simeon's wonder and blessing as he cradled the Christ child, calling Him "a light to bring revelation to the Gentiles, And the glory of Your people Israel" (Luke 2:32, *NKJV*). Jesus described Himself in terms of light. "Then Jesus spoke to them again, saying, *'I am the light of the world. He who follows Me shall not walk in darkness but have the light of life'" (John 8:12, NKJV).*

His light is so powerful that it pierces darkness; eradicates the penalty of sin for those who believe in Him; and provides a way for mankind to receive eternal life and redemption.

Shining the Light

We've established that Jesus is the Light, *but what does His light mean for the Church?*

If we are truthful, however, we must admit that we have not been very convincing light bearers. You probably haven't been and neither have I at times. Understanding what being the light means daily really can be difficult? Sometimes we confuse doing good works as being the only way we show people that we are the lights.

The good I do certainly can be one component of being a light but if people do not see Christ, then the things that I do are merely dead works without any eternal value.

The point of doing anything good should be so others may see our good deeds and glorify our Father in heaven" (Matthew 5:16, *NIV*). It is not about being recognized and applauded by others. We may be the doers, but the glory receiver, must be God. Although shining our light may at times be about what we do, it also must be about the kind of life I live. Shining Christ's light in the world means living my life in a way that others see Christ. Can I just will myself to do this right living? Absolutely not. It takes reliance on God's transformative power. It takes washing, and sanctification, and justification by the Spirit of our God and His Word. *These are the things that enable one to walk in the light day-by-day and to become increasingly effective as one of Christ's lights of the world (1 Corinthians 6:11, NKJV).*

Jesus' words in Matthew 5 say it all. Because we are in Him, He calls us to be His lights in this present world. *He made us light-bearers, and so each day we carry His light to the world. As carriers of His light we have the capacity to pierce darkness so that His light shines brightly through us so that the world may see, and be drawn to, Him.*

Because He has chosen us to be not only His messengers but His vessels, we should live as people of the light. As Paul wrote to the church of Corinth:

> *Remember, our message is not about ourselves; we're proclaiming Jesus Christ, the Master. All we are His messengers, errand runners from Jesus for you. It started when God said, 'Light up the darkness!' and our lives filled up with light as we saw and understood God in the face of Christ, all bright and beautiful.*
>
> *If you only look at us, you might well miss the brightness. We carry this precious message around in the unadorned clay pots of our ordinary lives. That's to prevent anyone from confusing God's incomparable power with us (2 Corinthians 4:5-7, MSG).*

No matter how beautiful we are on the outside that may draw attention to us, nothing is comparable to glory of His light that shines brightly through us that draws others into the presence of the Lord and grace of God.

Back on Track

It's important also that we do not allow anything to divert people's attention away from Jesus. We must examine our motives so that we never seek to take the place of Christ—the true and only Light. We must come to understand as John the Baptist did that we aren't the Light (John 1:6-9) but we are to bear witness of the Light.

How do we shine brightly with the Light of Christ? It starts with surrendering our lives to Him. Surrendering is not reserved for unbelievers only, but for believers as well. As we abide in Him, His Word abides in us and when we yield our lives to the control of the Holy Spirit, God's light will shine brighter through us. Daily, we will see our lives being transformed into His likeness- in the way we think, speak, act, and then we know what is good and pleasing to God (Romans 12:2; James 1:19-25). As we continue to surrender ourselves over to the Holy Spirit daily, we will see the character of Christ formed in us.

Remember, people are always watching how we live out our lives. They observe how we speak, think, notice our character, behavior, and how we respond to the issues of life. The world is waiting for us to do something about this darkness that they are experiencing. We are here to show them the light- to light up the world! The night is far spent, the day is at hand. Therefore, let us cast off the works of darkness, and let us put on the armor of light. (Romans 13:12)

Finally, let us not forget this. We have abiding in us this glorious Light of Christ waiting to shine brightly through us that the world may see and know Him. This Light in us is powerful enough to change the moral character of our nation, communities, families and church. This Light has the capability of bringing reformation, transformation, and hope to those living in darkness. *As His Lights we are the world's hope.*

Are you ready to rise and shine for all see that God's glory is upon you? Are you ready to be a light for the Light of the world? Are you ready to let God's Light shine through you?

Epilogue
God's Kingdom Unveiled

The primary reason Jesus came to earth was to inaugurate the Kingdom of God. Often, we hear that the reason Jesus came to the earth was to die on the Cross. Jesus did come to die on the Cross, but that death on the Cross was for the purpose of establishing the Kingdom of God.

John Eckhardt

No matter what the current circumstances—a church divided, a people divided, a world divided—God's kingdom will be established. The Church of Jesus Christ, the *ecclesia*, "the called-out people" will arise. I'm not speaking about the church that you attend on Sundays, the physical structure, or your denomination or congregation affiliation. I'm speaking about the Church of the Son of God. Jesus Himself said He was building His Church upon the rock and that even hell could not defeat it (Matthew 16:18). I'm speaking about the Church that Christ purchased with His very blood, we His people.

We Are the Church

Christ intends for us to arise. He gave Himself for us, to make us whole, radiant, pure, and blameless (Ephesians 5:25-27). He intends for His Church—His people—to shine like that city set on a hill for all to see His

Glory (Matthew 5:14-16). When we rise up, we lift Him up and draws others to Himself through the power of the Holy Spirit (John 12:32).

In the midst of darkness and chaos, in our world, America and in the life of the Church, the Church of Jesus Christ will arise. We do not have to worry about the present shaking. We are being pruned to bear much fruit. We are being cleaned up. The trash and debris burned up, so that all that remains is God. Then Christ glorious church will arise to be bright lights shining through the darkness to pave the way for the coming of our King and Lord. So, if God must shake us and everything around us- to wake us up to righteousness, He will.

God's plans for His Church will not be aborted, for Christ is alive in us. We will arise and become a triumphant and unified people—the glorious Church for which Christ will one day return.

The things that are happening in our world are nothing new. As we search Scripture, the things that are happening resemble things that happened in the past. Men were lovers of themselves, committing every imaginable type of sin and abomination, as they are today. Scripture tells us that there is nothing new under the sun (Ecclesiastes 1:9). However, amid darkness, the Israelites received a word from the Lord through Isaiah, which is relevant for us as well.

> *Arise, shine, for your light has come, and the glory of the LORD rises upon you. See, darkness covers the earth and thick darkness is over the people, but the LORD rises upon you and His glory appears over you. Nations will come to your light, and kings to the brightness of your dawn (Isaiah 60:1-3, NIV).*

We are in a better position than the Israelites were in Isaiah's day, because we have the light of Christ, and the deposit of His Spirit in us. With God's Spirit in us and upon us, surely, we can rise and shine and let the world experience the God we serve. We can serve as Christ's Light in the world. And, even if God must shake us, and everything around us, to wake us up, He will. The bottom line is this. God will have a people who will live their lives in such a way, that His glory will be revealed.

Unveiling God to the World

We have been made Christ's messengers to the world (Matthew 28: 19-20). Paul plainly tells us that, we are therefore Christ's ambassadors, as though God were making His appeal through us" (2 Corinthians 5:20, *NIV*). However, an ambassador is to represent well the one who sends him. So, how do we represent God well?

First, we must be willing to change our spiritual clothing. We must let go of, take off, our old ways that were planted in ignorance, blindness, and past sinfulness. When we came to Christ, that old life was supposed to be finished and our new life began (Ephesians 4:17-19). We put on Christ's clothing, character and nature. Scripture says this.

Since you have heard about Jesus and have learned the truth that comes from him, throw off your old sinful nature and your former way of life, which is corrupted by lust and deception. Instead, let the Spirit renew your thoughts and attitudes. Put on your new nature, created to be like God—truly righteous and holy. (Ephesians 4:21-24, NIV).

Is this easy to do? Yes … and no.

Yes, it is easy because Christ has already and completely removed the penalty of sin for us. The moment we accept Christ, we become new creations; old things have passed away and all things have been made new (2 Corinthians 5:17). It's done.

On the other hand, challenges persist. Although Christ's *salvation* work for us is completed, His *sanctification* work in us is ongoing; the realization of that new life is a continuing process, not something that happens overnight. There is molding and making that occurs, as God shapes us in the image of Christ. We need not worry that we are beyond God's transformative power, though. Scripture tells us that, we can be confident that because His Spirit abides in us, He who began a good work in us will carry it through to completion

(Philippians 1:6). *We already have the new life of Christ in us. As if we let go of our old life, we will see God's Spirit at work in us fashioning us after Himself.* If we choose to hold on to our old lifestyles, however, we cannot expect transformation to take place. And, without that transformation, we are unable to rise and to shine brightly to advance the Great Commission and point the world to Christ.

No matter what you might experience when you attend your home church or see happening in other churches around the world, confusion, sin or the lack of love, *God does have an army that is committed, devoted, and determined to make Jesus known to the world.* These are not wedded to the world's culture or traditions, but whose eyes are focused on King Jesus. *They may not wear the garb of a pastor, or be well-educated, or have a familiar name, but their names are written in the Lamb's Book of Life and they are the Church for which Christ will return.*

They have their eyes fixed on Jesus, the author and finisher of their faith. They come from every nation of the world and from every walk of life. They are strong in the Lord and filled with the Holy Spirit. They are proclaiming the gospel with boldness to anyone in their path. They are joining Christ in His work—feeding the poor, being surrogate fathers and mothers, attending to the sick. They are Christ's ministers of reconciliation—seeking to break down barriers both inside and outside of the church. They take seriously what they have been authorized to do by Christ, and sent out, to proclaim the good news of the gospel. While others are sleeping, they are alert and praying, piercing the darkness with the light of Christ's glory. They stand undeterred looking unto to Jesus, the Author and Finisher of their faith. They are world changers, carrying Christ's presence and power to our world. And, they invite you to join them.

Dear friends, our Great Commission assignment is a high calling. It is more than amassing people in a building; more than singing songs; or more than positioning stickers on cars, Bible on tables, or crosses around necks. *We—Christ's Church—are here for one purpose only, and that is to aid Him in establishing His kingdom of righteousness on earth as it is in heaven.* We must remember that we are not of the world's kingdom or government; we are of Christ's kingdom. We are His ambassadors, and our job is to inform the world about Him and His agenda. When we accepted Christ and His finished work, we became children of God; *we were enrolled as citizens of His kingdom, responding to our King's command.*

Believers and the world alike are waiting for us, to the manifest the Kingdom of God in the earth. Believers are waiting for the Church of Jesus Christ to stand up for truth, righteousness and walk in unity. Local churches are waiting for religion, traditions of men, dogmas and doctrines to be left behind and for Christ to be exalted. They also are waiting for Christ's Church, and the Kingdom of God to be unveiled. All around us, we see creation, believers and unbelievers crying out for redemption and freedom from death, decay, chaos, confusion and destruction- the consequences of sin. They are waiting for us to show them the glorious freedom that is in Christ Jesus and His glory. As Christ's Church, the redeemed, we have been given the charge to unveil Christ to the world. Christ's glory has entered and filled us, we are now one with Him, the Father and Holy Spirit. We belong to the family of God. We have what it takes to change the fabric of the world because the power of God has been made available to us. In the midst of darkness, we have been empowered by Christ's Spirit to be the lights of this world. We have the answer and the wisdom of God to address the problems that the world faces today. We have the mind of Christ, His thoughts, intent, and know the purpose of His heart. The world is waiting for us.

We must not ever forget our purpose and the mission that has been set before us. We do not have heaven to worry about because we have eternal life through Christ. We are a purpose driven people. We are not weaklings, but people who are strong in the Lord and have access to the power of God, the power greater than anything in this world. It is time that we step up and step out of our comfort zones, and boldly present to the world Christ, His Kingdom and to be the visible manifestation of His Kingdom on earth. We are here to extend to others an invitation to God's Kingdom through Christ, our Lord.

What about You?

I hope you are willing to embrace this high calling. Will you arise and be be the lights of Christ and pierce the darkness of this world? Will you give the Holy Spirit His rightful place and allow Him to fulfill His ministry in you and the local church? Will you sell out for God and leave your egos and agendas at the foot of the Cross? Will you take up the mantle of the Ambassador and live a righteous life so that others will be drawn to Christ? *I hope the answer is yes to all of these.*

As you prepare to move forward, allow me to offer a few notes of encouragement.

- *Pursue God and seek to please Him only.* Make God your first love and keep your eyes on Him (Revelation 2:4). As we see throughout Scripture, because we are imperfect beings, everyone messes up from time-to-time. However, make it your goal, and keep it front and center, to please the Father.

- *Be full of the Holy Spirit.* Yield yourself and control to the Holy Spirit. Allow Him to lead and guide you. Invite Him into your decision making and return the ministry of the Church to Him. After all, He has been designated as and is now the chief administrator of Christ's Church. Make time for Him and give the Spirit free reign in your life.

- *Surrender your will and plans to God.* Lay down your ego, self-righteousness, and self-centeredness. Remember that it is only through Him that you move, live, and have your being (Acts 17:28). When we surrender, we are relinquishing possession or control, and submitting our lives and plans over to the authority and control of God. We are in good company as this what Christ did for us. He abandoned His desires to fulfill the purpose, will and plan of His Father.

- *Walk in your authority.* Don't be a weakling, complaining about what you can't do and what Satan has done to you. Remember that only God is supreme; Satan can do nothing that God does not allow (Job 1:6-12). Further, you have been given authority over the devil and His activities. You are more than a conqueror, not because of your strength but through Him who loves us (Romans 8:37). The victory is always ours through Christ Jesus. It is not by our might or power, but by His Spirit, that we accomplish anything (Zechariah 4:6). We walk in victory because of Christ's victory, so we are strong in the Lord and His mighty power. He's given us His whole armor to use in this warfare (Ephesians 6:10-18)!

- *Pray without ceasing.* To live victoriously, communicating with God should a constant in the life of the believer. Even though God knows everything about us, we still are encouraged not to be anxious, but to pray continually, giving thanks in all circumstances (Philippians 4:6; 1 Thessalonians 5:17). God hears us. He knows our inner thoughts and our heart even before we pray. Prayer is one of the means created by God that He has given us to use to commune with Him -share with Him our innermost desires and needs.

- *Operate in the love of God.* Love is at the heart of God (1 John 4:8). It represents everything that He is and everything He has done for us. God has commanded us to love Him first and then our neighbors as ourselves. This doesn't mean that you always must love a person's behavior, but you are commanded to love the person as God has loved you (John 13:34). Rely on the Holy Spirit to help you love the way God does- unconditionally).

- *Remind yourself that you are in the world but not of the world.* Properly work within this world's system (Matthew 22:21; 1

Timothy 2:1-4), however, never forget Christ is your ultimate authority. We are not wedded to the world system or their ways of doing things. We are in this world to represent the King of Kings and His principles, standards and way of living.

- *Let nothing you do overshadow the gospel of Jesus Christ.* In everything, test your motives. Seek to ensure that you are advancing God's agenda instead of your own. Paul said this. But my life is worth nothing to me unless I use it for finishing the work assigned me by the Lord Jesus--the work of telling others the Good News about the wonderful grace of God. You and I also want nothing less than to be able to tell someone about Jesus and His work in our lives and the salvation that He brought to mankind. Our status, our position, or the possession of wealth should never overshadow the cause of Christ.

- *Never allow the culture of this world to diminish the gospel of Jesus Christ.* There is nothing in this world that has any eternal value. Their systems are corrupt, and built on lies, manipulation and profit. These can easily slip in to our lives and practices. So, we must be careful about what we hear, who we associate with and what practices we embrace that comes from the world's system. We must become diligent about the study of the Word, become accountable with mature believers, allow the Holy Spirit to guide our lives and activities, continually immerse ourselves in things that bring glory to God.

- *Recognize that any sort of division in the body is an affront to God.* God's vision of His body is of one that walks in unity. There is one body and one Spirit (Ephesians 4:1-6). Any "ism" that seeks to infiltrate the body must be removed. If you find yourself engaging in thought or activities that separate us from one another, repent, and then ask God to purify your heart so that you may walk in unity. Understand that division, contention, envy, jealousy, competition and confusion come from the evil one, Satan. Christ is not divided and neither does He intend for His Church to be. Also, God is not the author of confusion, Satan is.

- *Mature in behavior.* Throughout the New Testament, God inspired the writers to help us learn in practical ways how to act and live like His redeemed children. You don't expect a 50-year-old person to act like one who is 25, or 15, or 5. Similarly, as you grow in Christ, you also should see your character evolving. You want your behavior to mature daily so that, by nature, you find yourself doing what pleases the Father.

- *Understand that you may face opposition.* As you walk and witness for Christ, not everyone will appreciate you. When Jesus sent out the twelve disciples, He forewarned them that they wouldn't be received everywhere they went. In fact, He gave them permission to shake the dust from their feet when leaving a place where they were unwelcomed (Matthew 10:11-15). Jesus knows that we will not always get the response we desire. Keep praying and keep living in love … whatever the reaction. It is up to us simply to plant the seed and water it well; it is God who does the work in the heart and transforms a life (1 Corinthians 3:5-9).

- Choose to live a lifestyle of worship. Know that worship is more than a song or sermon, it is about the life we live. It is about Who God is, who we are and how we respond. It is allowing God place in us a heart of worship, one in which our thirst is for Him above anything or anybody.

In closing, know the harvest is ready. We have work to do. We have the gospel to proclaim, souls to be redeemed and the ever-growing body of Christ-to be discipled and equipped. Are you ready to unveil God's Kingdom to the world?

References

1. Revival Ministries International, God's Glorious Church, Published, 9/11/16
2. Crosswalk.com, Power of a Praying Church, Debbie Przybyiski, April, 27, 2015
3. Bible.org, How to Maintain Unity in the Church, Bible Teacher's Guide, Gregory Brown, 2005 F
4. First Adventures in Missions, Jesus 'Model of Discipleship, 2005
5. Adam Stadmiller, Christianity Today, The Prayer-Centered Church, What it takes to lead a prayerful community,, 2014
6. Jennie McChargue, Rock this Revival, 2018 Conference, Prayers You Should be Praying, Pt 2,, January 2018
7. West Stranberg- Michaelson Washington Post, Acts of Faith, I Think Christianity is dying? No, Christianity is Shifting Dramatically, May 20, 2015
8. Institute in Basic Life Principles, Why did God give us spiritual gifts?, Key Purpose for Spiritual Gifts-Edifiying the Church, Bringing glory to God, 201
9. Ray Pritchard, Chritsianity.com, The Great Commission: Does It Still Matter
10. John Piper, Desiring God, I am the Light of the World, May 12, 2011
11. Tony Evans, The Mystery and Mission of the Body of Christ, God's Glorious Church,
12. Jonathan Walton and Kin Wies, The Advancing Kingdom
13. Brian Houston, Hillsong, For This I Was Born

14. Darrel and Cindy Deville, God's Answer for America
15. Richard Warmbrand, John Piper, Milton Marvin, The Triumphant Church.
16. Kay Arthur, The Holy Spirit Unleashed in You
17. Ira Milligan, The Church Triumphant, Strategies for War
18. Christina Cleveland, Disunity in Christ, Uncovering the Hidden Forces That Keep Us Again,
19. David S. Anderson, Gracism, The Art of Inclusion
20. Sid Roth, The Incomplete Church, Bridging the Gap Between God's Children
21. Frederick K.C. Price, D.D, Race Religion& Racism, A Bold Encounter with Division in the Church
22. Darrell Guder, *Missional Church*
23. James McDonald, Walking in Unity
24. Frances Dixon, Walk Worthy of the Calling
25. Modern Problems, Biblical Answers, Denominationalism, Annual Preachers Files Lectureship

SCRIPTURE READINGS BY CHAPTER

Introduction

Amos 3:7, Ezekiel 3:17, Isaiah 62:6, Ezekiel 33:6, Matthew 28:19-20, Matthew 22:37-39.

Chapter 1   Everything Is Being Shaken … until All that Remains Is of God

Hebrews 12:25-29, MSG, John 16:33, Matthew 4:18-20, Luke 19:12-13

Chapter 2   Hindrances to Fulfilling the Great Commission

Matthew 28:18-20, John 14:12-18

Chapter 3   Neglect of One of Our Greatest, Gift, The Holy Spirit: (Hindrance #1)

Mark 1:9-11, John 14:12, John14:15-17, Acts 1:4-5, 2:1-4a, John 14:12, Acts 2:38-39, Genesis 1:2, John 14:26, 15:26, John 16:1, John 16:13-14, Acts 1:8, Acts 16:6-7, Acts 2:6-12. Acts 2, 1 Corinthians 12 and 14 Ephesians 4:30. Galatians 5:16-26; Ephesians 4:25-32, Romans 12:3-8

Chapter 4   No Prayer, No Power (Hindrance #2)

Isaiah 56:7, Isaiah 55:9; Matthew 26:36-46, Romans 8:15, Galatians 4:6).2 Samuel 5:17-21 (NKJV), (Psalm 34:4), (2 Samuel 12:16), Samuel 13:14, Acts 13:22, Mark 1:35, Matthew 14:23, Luke 6:12-13, Luke 22:44, (Matthew 6:5-15, Acts 1:12-14, 2:1-4. Acts 2:41, Acts 9:10-12, Acts 12:5-11, Acts 12:5-112, Chronicles 7:14, James 5:16-18, 1 John 5:14-15, Jeremiah 29:12, Colossians 4:2, 1 Thessalonians 5:17). (Hebrews 4:14-16, from 2 Chronicles 7:14, James 5:16, Ephesians 6:18, 1 Corinthians 12:10, 1 Corinthians 14:2, 1 Corinthians 12:6, 1 Corinthians 14:6-40, 1 Corinthians 14:26-2, 1 John 5:14-15

Chapter 5   A House Divided Cannot Stand (Hindrance #3)

Matthew 12:25, NKJV, 1 Corinthians 1:10-13, 1 Corinthians 1:17, Ephesians 4:3 John 17: 20-23, Ephesians 4:1-6, NIV

Chapter 6   Culture Mix-Up (Hindrance #4)

John 17:14-16; 1 John 2:1. Romans 12:2, NIV, Mark 16:15, John 17:14, NKJV. 1 Peter 2:7-8, 1 John 2:15-17, 1Timothy 2:1-3 Ephesians 6:13. 2 Corinthians 4:2-6, 2 Corinthians 5:20, Mark 16:15

Chapter 7   My Skin is … : Racism and Acceptance (Hindrance #5)

Matthew 28:19, Mark 16:15, John 4:3-4, John 4:7-41, Acts 2:7-11, Acts 2:41, NKJV). Galatians 2:11-16, Galatians 3:26-28, Romans 12:3, John 8:50. Ephesians 4:30-32, 1 John 4:7-8). 1 John 2:9-11, Galatians 6:10, NIV, Revelation 7:9, Matthew 6:10. John 1:12, Romans 2:11, John 13: 34-35, NIV.

Chapter 8   Fear vs. Boldness in Proclaiming the Gospel (Hindrance #6)

Deuteronomy 31:1-6), Deuteronomy 31:7-8; Joshua 1:1-9, Psalm 23:4-5, 27:1-3Matthew 1:20; Luke 1:3), Matthew 10:26-28, 14:27; Luke 5:10, 12:7; John 14:27. Matthew 1:20; Luke 1:30). Matthew 10:26-28, 14:27; Luke 5:10, 12:7; John 14:27. Acts 18:9. 27:23-26,2 Timothy 1:7, Acts 2:14-39, 3:11-26, 4:8-13. Luke 24. John 14:6, Philippians 4:13, Philippians 1:6, John 15:18-19, 16:33,

Chapter 9   Missing Component: Making Disciples (Hindrance #7)

John 3:3, Luke 6:40, (John 13:12-17, John 5:19-20, Luke 9:23, NIV, Luke 14: 26, Mark 10:28-30. (Acts 17:28). (John 15:4; 1 John 2:24), Matthew 28:19-20, 2 Timothy 4:2, 1 Corinthians 13:11, 1 Corinthians 3:5-8

Chapter 10   Satan: The Author of Division (Hindrance #8)

1 Peter 5:8), Isaiah 14:12-14, Revelation 12:7-9. Genesis 3:1-6; 1 Chronicles 21:1; Job 1:6-12; Matthew 4:1-11; Mark 8:33; John 13:27; Acts 5:3; 1 Timothy 1:20. 1 John 3:8, John 8:44, John 10:10, NIV, John 12:31, 16:11, 1 Corinthians 15:54-57. Isaiah14:15-19, Revelation 20:10, Judges 7:19; 2 Samuel 13:34; 2 Chronicles 23:6; Nehemiah 4:9; Matthew 24:42-44; Mark 1 3:34; 1 Corinthians 16:13; 2 Timothy 4:5,2 Corinthians 11:13-15, John 10:1-30, John 15, Mark 4:1-20, Ephesians 6:10-17, NIV. Matthew 4:1-11. Luke

10:19; John1:1-2, 1 Peter 5:8, John 8:31-32, Luke 10:39. John 15:1-8. 1 John 2:6, John 15:5, Ephesians 6:10-17, Romans 8:37. Romans 16:19, Psalm 100:3. 2 Chronicles 20:15. Isaiah 35:4.1 Peter 3:14, 1 John 4:4, Matthew 16:18.

Chapter 11   Without Love (Hindrance #9)

(1 Corinthians 13:1-7, 1 Corinthians 13:4-7, John 3:16, Romans 5:8, Romans 8:14-17, John 15:9, Psalm 23, Romans 8:28-29; 1 Corinthians 6:11. Matthew 22:38-39, Luke 19:1-10, Luke 18:15-17), (John 11:1-37). (John 13:34-35, 1 Corinthians 13:1, Romans 8:35-39, 2 Corinthians 13:5, Romans 5:8, John 15:9, John 15:1-17. Galatians 5:22-23, Matthew 5:13-16, Galatians 6:10, Matthew 5:43-48, 1 Corinthians 13:8, John 15:9-10. Jude 20-21, John 14:12-14, 1 John 4:7-8,

Chapter 12   Called to Light up the World with the Light of Christ

Matthew 5:13-16, Genesis 1:2-5, Exodus 13:21-22, Psalm 119:105, Isaiah 2:5, John 1:4-5, Matthew 4:16, Luke 2:32, (John 8:12, Matthew 5:16, 1 Corinthians 6:11, John 8:12. Revelation 3:20, Romans 12:2; James 1:19-25, 1 Corinthians 6:9-11, Philippians 3:13-14,

EPILOGUE   God's Kingdom Revealed

Ephesians 4:17-19, Ephesians 4:20-24, 2 Corinthians 5:17, Psalm 34:8,1 John 4:13-16, Revelation 2:4, Acts 17:28, Job 1:6-12, (Romans 8:37), Zechariah 4:6, Ephesians 6:10-18, Philippians 4:6; 1 Thessalonians 5:17, Jeremiah 29:11, John 13:33,1 John 4:8, I John 13:35, Matthew 22:21; 1 Timothy 2:1-4.

About the Author

Jocelyn Whitfield is a prolific author who uses the pen to challenge the hearts and minds of people to embrace the abundant life that God promises in Christ. She not only writes about spiritual interests but also takes on topics that are sometimes uncomfortable and controversial; with the hope that these discussions will spur believers and others to action to address real-life issues facing people in our world.

She is also a speaker, bible teacher, conference convener and has established faith and community coalitions across the country to address community problems.

Jocelyn's books: *The Better than Abundant Life, Doing Life God's Way, Women of Faith Living their Dreams, Still Slaves in America, Working Together Breaking the Chains of Poverty,* and *Change Your Words- Change Your Life.*

You may contact Jocelyn at jocelyn7266@gmail.com

Printed in the United States
By Bookmasters